YOU ARE SHERLOCK HOLMES

Published in 2023 by Welbeck,
an imprint of Welbeck Non-Fiction Ltd,
part of Welbeck Publishing Group.
Based in London and Sydney.
www.welbeckpublishing.com

A CIP catalogue record for this book is
available from the British Library

ISBN: 978 1 80279 425 0

Editor: Conor Kilgallon
Designer: Eliana Holder
Illustrations: Intrepidbooks.co.uk

Printed in Dubai

10 9 8 7 6 5 4 3 2 1

YOU ARE

SHERLOCK HOLMES

RICHARD WOLFRIK GALLAND

WELBECK

CONTENTS

INTRODUCTION

In 1887 Sir Arthur Conan Doyle introduced readers to the world's greatest fictional detective, Sherlock Holmes, whose adventures are recorded in four novels and 56 short stories.

The adventures in this volume are based on three short stories that were first published in *The Strand Magazine* and later compiled in *The Adventures of Sherlock Holmes* and *The Memoirs of Sherlock Holmes*.

The original stories were, of course, narrated by Holmes's friend and companion Dr John Watson. We saw Holmes's genius through Watson's eyes and his powers of deduction seemed like magic until he deigned to explain them, whereupon the doctor would invariably remark how simple it all seemed.

In this book YOU are Sherlock Holmes and the outcome of each adventure is in your hands. When directed, turn to the numbered section shown and continue reading; when you

are given a choice, turn to the numbered section that matches your preferred option. A word to the wise: *Remember that each case stands on its own two feet.* An instruction to 'Go to Section 34', for example, relates to that case only.

You must employ observation and reason to solve the cases. A familiarity with Conan Doyle's original works may help you, but you should not be complacent.

Some threads will allow you to stay true to the original story, while others will take you in completely new directions. Will you prove to be as successful as the Great Detective or will you fall short of his genius? Even Holmes sometimes failed to resolve a case. Perhaps you think you can do better...

A note about *The Final Problem*. In the short story Conan Doyle was determined to kill off our hero once and for all. To retain the spirit of the original (before the author was compelled to resurrect Holmes a decade later), there are several routes that will lead to your gruesome demise. You have been warned!

A SCANDAL IN BOHEMIA

1

It is March 1888 and London is experiencing a peculiarly dry start
to the Spring. Across the Atlantic, the denizens of New York, New
Jersey and New England are in the grip of a severe blizzard.

You look up from the evening paper's meteorological report,
alerted to the sound of familiar footsteps outside. Moments later
your colleague Dr John Watson appears. It has been some time
since you last saw one another and you feel an irresistible impulse
to provoke him.

'Wedlock suits you, Watson. I think you have put on seven and a
half pounds since I saw you.'

'Seven!' he replies indignantly.

'Indeed, I should have thought a little more. And you are in
practice again, I observe.'

'How on Earth can you have deduced that?'

'I see it, I deduce it. In the same way I can deduce that you have
been getting yourself very wet lately, and that you have a most
clumsy and careless servant.'

Watson smiles, 'Holmes you would have been burned as a
warlock had you lived two centuries ago! Please explain.'

'Simplicity itself. You have a distinct odour of iodoform, a
black mark of nitrate of silver on your right forefinger
and a bulge on the right side of your top-hat
where you secreted your stethoscope.
On the inside of your left shoe the
leather is scored by six almost
parallel cuts, caused by someone
who has very carelessly scraped
round the edges of the sole in
order to remove crusted mud
from it.'

'It always seems so ridiculously simple when you explain it, that I could easily do it myself and I believe my eyes are as good as yours.'

'You see, but you do not observe,' you reply. Aware that you are lecturing, you soften your tone and hand him a letter. 'Perhaps you could apply my methods to this, it arrived by the last post.'

There will call upon you to-night, at a quarter to eight o'clock, a gentleman who desires to consult you upon a matter of the very deepest moment. Your recent services to one of the royal houses of Europe have shown that you are one who may safely be trusted with matters which are of an importance which can hardly be exaggerated. This account of you we have from all quarters received. Be in your chamber then at that hour, and do not take it amiss if your visitor wears a mask.

Watson reads the letter carefully and shakes his head. 'This is indeed a mystery, what do you imagine it means?'

'The content tells us very little, but there is more to be learned from this letter. The handwriting reveals that it was written by a man, a German judging by the verbal structure. Now hold the paper up to the light, there is a maker's mark which tells us that it was made in Bohemia.'

Your analysis is interrupted by the sound of hooves and wheels, coming to a halt directly outside.

☛ *It appears your visitor has arrived. Meet them at Section 2.*

2

'I think that I had better go, Holmes.' suggests Watson.

You shake your head emphatically. This will be a perfect opportunity to educate the doctor in the art and science of observation and, besides, he could be of some use. The visitor rings the bell and is shown up to your room by a bedazzled Mrs Hudson.

He is six feet tall and heavily muscled with a proud bearing and equally ostentatious attire. Heavy bands of astrakhan are slashed across the sleeves and fronts of his double-breasted coat, and his deep blue cloak is lined with flame-coloured silk and secured at the neck with a brooch in the shape of a golden chalice. Boots trimmed with rich brown fur adorn his feet. His patrician face is obscured by a black velvet mask.

'You had my note?' he asks in a deep, accented voice, German just as you suspected. 'I told you that I would call.' He looks from you to Watson, uncertain who to address.

You offer the visitor a seat, introduce yourself and your colleague, and wait for him to reciprocate.

'You may address me as the Count Von Kramm,' he says, 'and I should much prefer to communicate with you alone.'

Watson rises to leave but you push him back into his seat. It is time to take control of the situation. 'You may say before this gentleman anything which you may say to me.'

'Very well,' responds the visitor, 'but I must bind you both to absolute secrecy for two years; at the end of that time the matter will be of no importance. At present, however, it may have an influence upon European history.'

Watson promises without hesitation, and you give your word without attempting to disguise your amusement. However, entertaining as this charade may be, you think it better if you disabuse your visitor of the notion that his mask and alias are an obstacle to your powers of deduction.

'Please take a seat, Your Majesty.'

The effect of your words on the visitor is most satisfying. He appears ready to offer a red-faced denial, but you administer the coup de grace:

'I believe I am addressing Wilhelm Gottsreich Sigismond von Ormstein, Grand Duke of Cassel-Felstein, and hereditary King of Bohemia?'

The King removes his mask dramatically. He is clearly not a man used to being outmanoeuvred but takes the proffered seat and prepares to deliver his monologue.

☞ *To hear your regal client's story,*
go to Section 7.

3

Your powers of observation are in fine fettle today. You will need them to fool the *Illuminati*.

The cab drops you off in Hampstead. As you walk towards Camden Town, an idea starts to form.

CAMDEN TOWN
LONDON BOROUGH OF CAMDEN   NW1

☛ *Go to Section 22.*

4

The following morning you take toast and coffee with Watson while you await the arrival of the King. When His Majesty arrives, you take his private carriage to Briony Lodge.

The King is overjoyed that you have located the photograph, but you feel something is amiss when you arrive at Briony Lodge, to find the door open and an elderly woman standing upon the steps.

'Mister Sherlock Holmes, I believe?' she asks.

'I am he,' you reply.

'My mistress told me that you were likely to call. She wished me to convey that she left this morning with her husband by the five-fifteen train from Charing Cross for the Continent. Never to return.'

The King gasps, 'But what of the papers? All is lost!'

You push past the servant, enter the sitting room, and open the secret compartment in the fireplace. It contains a photograph and a single letter. The photograph is of Irene alone and the note is addressed to you.

☞ ◬ *To read the letter, go to*
Section 51.

5

The driver looks askance at your attire, but any objection is silenced when you show him some coin.

'The Church of Saint Monica and half a sovereign if you reach it in twenty minutes,' you command.

The cabby does not disappoint and sets off at a ferocious pace.

On arriving at the church, you find it all but empty; only Miss Adler, Mr Norton and a priest stand at the altar, apparently engaged in a restrained disagreement. As there is no law prohibiting it, you shuffle to a side aisle and take a pew, just close enough to overhear.

To your surprise the three figures turn to stare in your direction and Mr Norton rushes towards you. You look up, carefully maintaining the mannerisms of your disguise.

'Thank God,' says Norton. 'You'll do. Come, man, we only need three minutes, or it won't be legal!'

They want you to act as witness!

You have no option. If you wish to keep Irene Adler under surveillance, you will have to participate. The priest gives you some words to say and you repeat them in your ostler's voice, hoping that your reluctance to make eye contact is interpreted as class-conscious discomfort.

Finally, he pronounces the pair man and wife, and you are smothered with gratitude by Mr and Mrs Norton. The bride even gives you a sovereign for your trouble! Then you are forgotten as they hasten from the church to separate carriages.

Before they part ways you are able to overhear a brief exchange. She informs him that she intends to drive out this evening as usual.

☛ *If you want to pursue Godfrey Norton, go to Section 27.*

☛ *If you would rather leave them both for now and enlist some help, go to Section 22.*

6

On the way to Serpentine Avenue, you hastily explain your plan to Watson. It will require his medical expertise but only in a theatrical sense.

You find the normally tranquil street crowded and recognise almost everyone: the group of shabbily dressed men smoking in the corner, the scissors-grinder working at his wheel, two guardsmen flirting with a nurse, and several well-dressed young men lounging with cigars in their mouths, the actors have taken their positions.

The plan is perhaps too elaborate, but authenticity is everything. One of the scissor grinders knocks on the door of Briony Lodge and is answered by the housekeeper who tries to send him on his way. The tradesman's persistence becomes almost menacing, and he manages to wedge the door open before the stalwart servant can slam it in his face. Now you make your move.

'Now see here,' you admonish the man in your clergyman's voice.

'Mind your own business, preacher!' he turns on you and delivers a clout to the side of your head. You roll with the blow, which smarts nevertheless, and fall to the ground.

'Oh lord, he's killed 'im!' shouts one of your paid onlookers.

You hear footsteps approaching from all directions and a cacophony of dismay and concern. One voice rises above the din:

'Let me through, I am a doctor.'

You keep your eyes closed as Watson lifts your wrist and proclaims, 'I must get him inside!'

The good doctor's authority seems to overcome the housekeeper's propriety and you feel yourself lifted, carried and deposited onto an upholstered surface.

When you open your eyes, you and Watson are alone in Irene Adler-Norton's sitting room.

What is your plan?

☛ *Wait for Irene Adler to return home? Go to Section 50.*

☛ △ *Or have Watson search the room under your supervision? Go to Section 39.*

7

'Some five years ago, during a lengthy visit to Warsaw, I made the acquaintance of the well-known adventuress, Irene Adler. The name is no doubt familiar to you.'

It is not. You do not commit details about the rich and famous to memory unless they are pertinent to a case. However, you do keep an index of such personages. You ask Watson to find it and look her up. A minute later, he hands you a card:

> Irene Adler. Born: New Jersey 1858.
>
> Operatic career as a contralto. Performed at the La Scala in Milan and as prima donna in the Imperial Opera of Warsaw. Now retired from the operatic stage and residing in London.
>
> Briony Lodge, Serpentine Avenue, St. John's Wood.

You make a calculated guess: 'Your Majesty became entangled with Miss Adler, wrote her some compromising letters, and is now desirous of getting those letters back.'

'Precisely.'

'Letters can be forged, note paper stolen and royal seals imitated. Surely, she has nothing to threaten Your Majesty.'

'There is a photograph. A large, cabinet photograph.'

'Photographs can be bought.'

'We are both in the photograph.'

'Ah! Your Majesty has committed an indiscretion. Clearly it must be paid for or otherwise recovered.'

'She refuses to sell, and I have sent professional thieves on five separate attempts, all have failed.'

'If her objective is not extortion, what does she hope to do with the photograph?'

'She intends to ruin me. I am about to be married to Princess Clotilde Lothman von Saxe-Meningen of Scandinavia. If the indiscretion became known, her family would not permit the marriage to go ahead. Miss Adler has promised to send the photograph to the princess's family on the day our betrothal is officially announced.'

'And when is that?'

'Next Monday.'

'That should give us ample time,' you smile, 'We have only one other thing to discuss.'

The King nods. 'I would give one of my provinces to have that photograph.' He takes a leather bag from under his cloak and lays it on the table. 'There are three hundred pounds in gold and seven hundred in notes. I am currently staying in London at the Langham.'

Watson's eyes almost bulge from their sockets as you write out a receipt for the King.

☞ If you want to start your investigation at Irene Adler's London home, go to Section 15.

☞ If you want to enlist some local help, go to Section 10.

8

'And what of Miss Adler herself?' you ask.

'We spoke to some local lads what work at the stables. They said that she keeps herself to herself, hardly ever leaving the front sitting room, but she takes her carriage for a drive around the park every evening at five and she's always back at seven sharp for supper.'

'How accessible is Briony Lodge?'

'I wouldn't want to live there if I had anything of value. There's a stables round the back and ridiculous large windows on the ground floor that look straight into the street.'

'Are Mr and Mrs Norton at home now?'

'No, he's at his office, she's gone into town. Shouldn't think either will be back until evening.'

You reward Wiggins for his excellent reconnaissance and ponder your next move. It almost seems too easy.

☛ *If you want to head to Briony Lodge immediately and try to break in, go to Section 23.*

☛ *If you think there is a more subtle way to get into the house and discover the location of the photograph, go to Section 22.*

9

You send word to the King that you intend to visit Briony Lodge at eight o'clock tomorrow morning.

At 221b Baker Street, as you take out the keys to your door, a youth in an ulster passes by and wishes you a cheery 'Good-night, Mr Sherlock Holmes!'

Your reputation, it seems, continues to grow - is this a blessing or a curse?

☞ *If you return the salutation, go to Section 19.*

☞ *If you pretend that you did not hear, go to Section 4.*

10

The King of Bohemia may have paid bandits at his disposal, but you doubt any of his scouts are a match for your army of local urchins, the Baker Street Irregulars. You send for their leader, a needle-sharp young scoundrel by the name of Wiggins.

'I'd like you to watch a residence and report on anyone who goes in or out of it,' you command, giving Wiggins Miss Adler's address and some coins for his expenses. He responds with a cheeky salute and leaves to marshal his troops.

It is two o'clock in the afternoon the following day when Wiggins returns with some interesting news.

'The lady of the house got married at noon today, to a lawyer by the name of Sir Godfrey Norton. After they got hitched, Miss Adler - I mean Mrs Norton - came home but her new 'usband was nowhere to be seen.'

'Do you know where this Godfrey Norton resides?' you ask.

'No, but he works in the Temple with all them other legal folks,' Wiggins hands you a business card bearing Norton's name. You do not ask him how he obtained it.

'Excellent work. And would you recognise Mr Norton by sight?'

'I think so.'

> ☞ If you would like to investigate Godfrey Norton, go to Section 20.
>
> ☞ If you prefer to keep your attention on Irene Adler-Norton, go to Section 8.

11

No, you followed the obvious route. You need to check this location number against a number on the table in Section 54.

☞ *Try again. Return to Section 41.*

12

Having been forewarned of your adversary's powers of concealment, you are on your guard.

'Good-night,' you reply offhandedly, before dropping your keys and leaping at the youth, who attempts to flee a moment too late.

With your martial expertise and heavier physique, it seems to be no contest. However, the youth applies a desperate knee to a delicate part of your anatomy, and you are forced to release your grip.

The youth prepares to flee a second time but turns to find the blade of Dr Watson's sword-stick an inch from their trachea. The look on your colleague's face leaves no doubt that he is prepared to violate the Hippocratic Oath if needs must.

You grab one of the youth's slender wrists and drag the protesting figure into 221b Baker Street.

'Now Mrs Irene Norton, what business takes you away from the comfort of St. Johns Wood?' you ask.

Watson's eyes bulge incredulously as the youth removes her cap and shakes out a full head of lustrous hair. She stares at you, half-defiant, half-amused.

'I wanted to see the undisguised visage of the bloodhound Wilhelm had set on me.'

'Or perhaps that of your masters' new lapdog? I am no one's pawn, madame. Here are my terms: return to St. John's Wood, destroy the photograph and any other incriminating documents. Moreover, swear to be of no future hindrance to King Wilhelm of Bohemia, or I shall expose you and your organisation from Fleet Steet to the Vatican, am I clear?'

Irene Adler-Norton recoils and swallows several times. 'Perfectly clear.'

She carefully replaces her cap, then pushes past an astonished Watson and out the front door, disappearing into a crowd of similarly attired youths.

'That was ...?'

'A remarkable woman, Watson, playing a game with very high stakes indeed. Come, we must away to the Langham and convince a very unremarkable King that his honour is no longer in danger.'

THE END

13

The letter is an assurance of a permanent impasse. Irene declares that her love for Godfrey Norton will prohibit her from ever making the photograph public, not one but two marriages would be destroyed if it were to happen.

The King is not easily mollified but you are able to convince him of his position: if he moves to harm Irene Adler-Norton, she has the means to retaliate, but otherwise his honour is safeguarded.

You ask to keep the portrait by way of final payment for your services and the King consents dismissively.

When you return to Baker Street you take another look at the photograph. Turning it over you see a tiny hand-drawn pyramid, containing an eye, the symbol of the *Illuminati*. Did Irene know that you would ask for the print?

You sense that you have been manipulated by unseen forces throughout this case. Perhaps you have made some influential allies, but at what cost?

Putting the photograph into a drawer, you take up your pipe and look through the window into the London night. The flash of a match illuminates your refection in the pane, then the comforting darkness returns.

THE END

14

It is almost 5 o'clock in the evening when you take a spartan supper of cold beef and a glass of beer while relaying your adventures, and the rudiments of your plan, to Watson.

'Would you have any objection to breaking the law and running the chance of arrest?' you ask.

'Not in the least - if it were in a good cause.'

'Oh, the cause is excellent!' you cry, 'Madame will return to Briony Lodge at seven, we must be prepared.'

Your first step is to disguise yourself as a clergyman with a broad black hat, baggy trousers and a simple-minded countenance that brings a smile to Watson's face.

There are possible two ways to implement your plan.

☛ *If you choose to head back to Serpentine Avenue with all haste, go to Section 6.*

☛ *If you prefer to arrive at Briony Lodge just before seven o'clock, go to Section 18.*

The following morning at 8 o'clock, you leave Baker Street disguised as an unemployed groom and make your way on foot to St John's Wood. You use the half-hour walk to perfect your camouflage, changing your posture and gait to blend in with the city's fortuneless multitude.

Briony Lodge proves to be a compact but elegant two-storey villa directly accessible from the street. You had expected a fortress and are somewhat disappointed by the lack of external security; the front door has a Chubb lock, but the long ground-floor windows look particularly vulnerable.

You are able to walk around the house unchallenged. When you enter the lane that runs parallel to its rear gardens, you find, as expected, a stables where ostlers are going about their business.

Greeting the workmen in their vernacular, you offer your services. They look at you sceptically, but clearly see you as one of their own and set you to rubbing down the horses.

They are greatly appreciative of your speed and skill. After an hour's work you have been rewarded with some tobacco, a glass of ale and tuppence. Most importantly the men are more than happy to share what they know of Miss Irene Adler.

You learn that she drives out at five every evening and returns at seven for dinner. A cabman tells you that Miss Adler has a frequent visitor, a gentleman by the name of Godfrey Norton, a lawyer by profession. The cabman is in the process of furnishing you with some lurid speculation regarding their acquaintance when he stops suddenly and points at a hansom that has just pulled up outside Briony Lodge.

'That's the gentleman himself, right there!'

A handsome man alights from the cab, knocks on the front door, and disappears inside the villa. You catch glimpses of him

through the living room window, pacing, talking and gesticulating excitedly. About half an hour later he leaves the house and reboards the cab.

'Drive like the devil,' he shouts, 'first to Gross & Hankey's in Regent Street, and then to the Church of Saint Monica in the Edgware Road. Half a guinea if you do it in twenty minutes!'

The cab departs at speed and a moment later another takes its place and then you see her for the first time. The beautiful woman who hurries gracefully to the cab can only be Irene Adler.

'The Church of Saint Monica and half a sovereign if you reach it in twenty minutes,' she cries.

A third vacant cab turns into Serpentine Avenue. You look at your pocket watch, it is twenty-five minutes to twelve.

What will you do?

☞ *Hail the cab and go to the Church? Go to Section 5.*

☞ *Attempt to break into the house? Go to Section 23.*

A SCANDAL IN BOHEMIA

16

Excellent. You are mastering the skills of an Illuminatus. Take care not to alert King Wilhelm that you are no longer acting in his interests.

The cab drops you off near Camden Town, so you can stretch your legs and consider your next move.

☞ *Go to Section 22.*

A SCANDAL IN BOHEMIA

17

You hail the next available cab and direct it to Temple.

Less than an hour later you arrive in a district comprised almost entirely of law offices. It does not take long to locate the one indicated on Norton's business card.

Flipping the card over, you ponder the simple map. The lines certainly correspond to the surrounding streets and appear to link Norton's chambers with another location. Your instincts tell you it will yield more information than a lawyer's office.

Following a series of increasingly unsanitary lanes, you come to the location of the second X: an apparently derelict gothic building. Its front entrance is boarded up but there is a passage running alongside it, where a row of large planks have been propped up against the wall.

After ensuring that you are unobserved, you enter the lane and remove the planks to reveal a side door that is clearly still in use.

☛ *If you try the handle, go to Section 31.*

☛ *If you believe the photograph is somewhere else, go to Section 22.*

18

You explain your plan: 'I shall be conveyed into the house, and I must ask that you do nothing until this is accomplished. When I open the sitting room window, wait for my signal, and then throw this plumbers' smoke rocket inside, it is fitted with a cap at either end to make it self-lighting. Everyone has been instructed to raise a cry of fire, feel free to join them. Then walk to the end of the street and wait for me to join you. Is that clear?'

Watson simply nods and stares at the long cigar-shaped object that you have just handed to him.

You arrive with ten minutes to spare. The lamps are being lit as the daylight fades, but the street is bustling. A group of shabbily dressed men smoke in one corner, a scissors-grinder is working at his wheel, two guardsmen are flirting with a nurse-girl, and several well-dressed young men lounge up and down with cigars in their mouths. You recognise them all.

A look of doubt clouds Watson's features, 'Holmes, how will you find the photograph? The King sent gangs of burglars and recovered nothing.'

'I find your lack of faith... disappointing,' you reply in your clergyman's voice, 'the lady herself will show me.'

At that moment a landau trots into the avenue and pulls to a halt outside Briony Lodge. One of the shabbily-dressed men rushes to its door, evidently hoping to earn himself a coin. One of his compatriots has exactly the same idea and the two men collide. As Irene Adler-Norton

Irene Adler

steps from the carriage she finds herself in the centre of a violent brawl. This is your cue to enter stage left.

You attempt to protect the lady from the riot and your theatrical intercession earns you a cudgel blow to the side of the head. As your vision wobbles, you dimly recall telling the men to make it look convincing and then you fall to the ground with a pool of red liquid gathering beneath your face.

The sight of a man of God so poorly treated pacifies the crowd, some voice their concerns for your well-being while others marvel at your bravery. You hear Irene's voice, clear as a bell: 'Bring him into the sitting room.'

As you are gently lowered onto a sofa, you gasp, 'Please... I need air.'

A maid helpfully opens one of the large windows and you are able to gesticulate through it in what you hope appears to be delirium to those inside the house and an affirmative signal to Watson on the outside.

'Fire!' shouts a familiar voice from the Avenue and, at the same moment, the room is engulfed in smoke. The cry is quickly taken up by servants and onlookers. In the pandemonium, you keep your attention firmly fixed on the lady and you watch as she moves to the fireplace and opens a secret compartment.

'It's not a fire ma'am. Look, it's just smoke!' shouts the housekeeper, pointing towards the smouldering plumber's rocket.

What now?

☛ *If you want to slip away in the confusion, return to Baker Street and notify the King that you have located his photograph, go to Section 9.*

☛ ⚠ *If you would rather retrieve the contents of the secret compartment now, go to Section 44.*

33

19

'Good-night,' you reply with what you hope sounds like genuine warmth.

Watson raises an eyebrow, 'You are in good spirits tonight, Holmes,' he observes.

'Indeed,' you reply. But in that moment, you are filled with the conviction that you have missed something important.

☞ *You shake off the feeling and go to Section 4.*

20

You hail a cab, accompanied by young Wiggins and head for Temple. Godfrey Norton's workplace is an unremarkable lawyers' office in a district composed almost entirely of lawyers' offices.

The street is busy, and you bide your time in companiable silence until the dusk gathers and the lamps are being lit. A gentleman appears at the entrance.

'That's 'im.' says Wiggins.

'You've done a commendable job,' you tell the urchin, giving him another coin, 'please convey my gratitude to the Irregulars.'

Wiggins tips his cap and disappears into the crowd. Godfrey Norton makes his way up the street and you pursue him at an unhurried pace and an unobtrusive distance.

Eventually he comes to a gothic building that, to the untutored eye, appears boarded-up and derelict. Norton casts a look about him before slipping into its side entrance.

Godfrey Norton

☛ *If you continue to follow Godfrey Norton, go to Section 31.*

☛ *If you have a better plan, one that doesn't involve strange old buildings, go to Section 22.*

21

The 'letter' is simply a drawing of an eye contained within a pyramid, the symbol of the Bavarian *Illuminati*. Without words, they have sent you a clear message: they are watching.

You feel the King's eyes burning into you.

'You have failed.' He says, like a judge pronouncing a capital sentence.

'Your Majesty should know that he has an adversary far more troublesome than a jealous paramour. There is a revolutionary organisation that seeks to destroy you.'

'What on Earth are you talking about?'

You indicate the chalice-shaped brooch at his neck. 'It is an organisation that takes exception to your beliefs.'

The King's face becomes a cold mask. 'Yes. There are those who deny the divine right of kings. But a reckoning is coming for them, just as it came to those who gave their name to your city's legal district.'

He is referring to the Knights Templar, burned at the stake almost six centuries ago by Philip IV and a Pope Clement V. The look of fury that twists the King's features tells you that he is not being metaphorical. He sweeps from the room with the same pride that brought him to your Baker Street home.

It seems you have earned the animosity of two mortal foes. Well, they say a man can be judged by the quality of his enemies.

THE END

22

An elaborate plan is taking root in your mind. You make your way to a tavern in Camden where you have made some curious acquaintances over the years. Your plan requires a crowd, and the inn has no shortage of volunteers, ready to perform street theatre for the price of a cup of gin.

When you have recruited a sufficiency of actors you decide to return home and prepare a suitable disguise for yourself. The question is: should you attempt to enter Briony Lodge while Irene Adler-Norton is taking her evening drive or wait until she returns?

☛ *While you are deciding, head back to Baker Street. Watson awaits you in Section 14.*

23

Breaking into a house full of servants in broad daylight will require a distraction. The steady clopping of a horse-drawn cab gives you an idea.

You ask the driver to wait outside and give him a more-than-generous portion of your expenses with the instruction, 'You are here to collect Mr Norton and must not budge until you have been paid.'

Then you knock on the door of Briony Lodge and step aside, flat to the wall. The door opens and you hear the housekeeper call imperiously, 'Yes?'

'I'm 'ere for Mr Norton!' shouts the cabbie, then repeats himself even louder.

The housekeeper rushes to the cab, as you hoped, eager to avoid any disturbance in her genteel domain. In that instant you slip inside, barely avoiding the vacant gaze of a serving girl as she descends the stairs and turns into the hallway.

You must admit, this is not one of your best-thought-out plans. But time is against you, and you need to find something useful. You enter the front sitting room, finding it empty.

'Noisy fool,' grumbles the housekeeper as she re-enters the house, evidently having paid off the cabbie.

'Will Miss Irene and Mr Norton be eating together when they return, Mrs Bridges?' The timid voice of the serving girl is just within earshot.

'I've told you already Nelly, it'll be Mr and Mrs Norton from now on. And no, he's going to his place in Temple.'

As their conversation fades, you survey the room. Everything is in good order; the fireplace has been cleaned recently and every surface polished. As you expected, the King's photograph is nowhere to be seen but a leatherbound book lies incongruously on a mahogany demilune table: *Kurze Rechtfertigung meiner Absichten*

by Adam Weishaupt. A card has been inserted as a bookmark; it belongs to Godfrey Norton and locates his chambers in New Square. On the back of the card are a series of hand-drawn lines that appear to connect two X's - a crude map perhaps?

As you are pondering this, you hear footsteps approaching from the hall. Pocketing the card, you open one of the large windows and let yourself out onto the street, an effective if undignified exit.

What now?

☞ *If you would like to visit Godfrey Norton's workplace, go to Section 17.*

☞ *If you believe the photograph is somewhere in Briony Lodge, go to Section 22.*

24

'That sounds eminently reasonable,' you reply.

You leave Briony Lodge and take a cab to the Langham to relay Irene's message to the King of Bohemia. He is not pleased but is eventually persuaded by the logic of it.

His wedding to Princess Clotilde Lothman von Saxe-Meningen of Scandinavia goes ahead without impediment and you are amply rewarded for your trouble.

You learn that Mr and Mrs Norton left St. John's Wood the day after your conversation. Perhaps that is the last you will hear of Irene Adler, a most formidable adversary, but you hope not.

THE END

25

'I will help you,' you reply tonelessly.

The mask seems to consider something, 'We do not ask much of you Sherlock Holmes, only that you continue to work for the King but, when your investigation is thwarted, you accept the outcome. Do this, and we promise that no one will be harmed.'

'That sounds very much like a threat.'

'Not at all, merely an assurance that your actions will bring no misfortune to any of the parties involved.'

☞ *If you still intend to work against the Illuminati, go to Section 41.*

☞ *If you have been persuaded to help them after all, go to Section 35.*

26

'*Lux in tenebris lucet*,' you reply and observe with satisfaction that the youth visibly stiffens before continuing down Baker Street with a less confident gait.

Watson raises an eyebrow, 'Holmes?'

'A snippet from the fifth verse of the first chapter of the Gospel of John,' you reply, 'and hopefully a reminder that we all must answer to someone.'

You are forced to admit that Irene Adler-Norton's mastery of disguise rivals your own. But, like you, she has a flare for the dramatic that could be her undoing.

☛ *You enter Baker Street with an unfamiliar but not unpleasant sensation. Go to Section 4.*

27

Fortunately, the cabbie who brought you to the church has stopped to take a meagre lunch and is waiting outside. You convince him that he can dine like a king if he will follow Norton's carriage to Temple. He swallows a last chewy morsel and complies with alacrity.

Following your advice, the driver keeps your quarry in sight while maintaining an unobtrusive distance. Less than an hour later, Norton is deposited outside one of Temple's many law offices but, as soon as his carriage has turned a corner, he turns on his heel and marches away from the legal district.

You pay your own cabbie and hasten after Godfrey Norton on foot, through a maze of increasingly unsavoury streets. As the crowds start to thin, you increase your distance. Eventually he arrives at a gothic building that appears boarded-up and derelict. Norton casts a look about him before slipping into its side entrance.

☛ *If you continue to follow Godfrey Norton, go to Section 31.*

☛ *If you would rather abandon your pursuit and plan a way to recover the photograph, go to Section 22.*

28

Pulling the hood over your head, you make for the source of the sinister dirge. As you get closer you can make out snatches of Latin, the word *lux* - 'light' - is intoned repeatedly.

You come to a heavy wooden door that has been left ajar; beyond it the sound is greatly amplified, but there is not enough light to see into the room. Steeling yourself, you slip inside but find you are still unable to discern anything.

Five paces into the shadowy chamber and you hear the door slam shut behind you. The chanting abruptly ends with the sound of a stylus scratching a gramophone.

Then you are blinded by a sudden explosion of light; someone has unhooded a blackout lantern.

'Welcome Sherlock Holmes,' says a masculine voice from the deepest shadow.

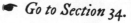

☞ *Go to Section 34.*

29

'I want no part in this,' you declare, 'your secrets can remain a secret, but I intend to proceed with the case as if this meeting had never happened.'

Your words are greeted with an ominous silence and then a cloud of dust explodes into the stream of lamplight. Before you can marshal your defences, you feel consciousness slipping away.

'That is a great pity, Sherlock Holmes,' says the masked voice, 'you would have made a fine illuminatus. We hold you to your promise - but know that we shall always be watching.'

You slip into the warm darkness and a swirl of strange dreams.

Another bright light assaults your eyelids, but this time it is daylight. You open your eyes tentatively and find yourself sitting on a park bench that you are sharing with a destitute old woman.

'Spare a farthing, dear?' she asks the moment you make eye contact.

You happily hand her one of your coins - she has given you an idea!

☞ *Get up and go to Section 22.*

30

You move to the fireplace and activate the secret compartment; it contains a photograph and a sheaf of letters. The photograph is well-taken, its depiction of the King and Irene Adler-Norton, unmistakable. There is no need to concern yourself with the content of the letters, you are certain that all the incriminating material is here.

The sound of a revolver being cocked shakes you from your analysis. Turning around, you are face to face with Mrs Irene Adler-Norton and a very proficiently wielded firearm.

You carefully replace the documents in the compartment and close the door. Irene Adler-Norton lowers her weapon, says simply, 'Good day to you father,' and allows you to leave by the front door.

☛ *It is time to inform the King that you have located his photograph. Go to Section 4.*

31

You try the door and find it unlocked. Opening it slowly there is only the faintest creak, but it still puts your nerves on edge. The interior is dimly illuminated by recently-lit candles placed at judicious intervals.

Following the flickering lights, you come to a cloakroom. There are five empty hooks and one on which hangs a garment resembling a monk's habit.

The sound of distant chanting carries eerily along the adjoining corridor. Something about the acoustics feels wrong.

In a situation like this you generally prefer to have Watson watching your back with a loaded pistol at the ready.

It's not too late to back out.

☛ *If you put on the monk's robe and follow the chanting, go to Section 28.*

☛ *If you think venturing into the shadows alone is a very bad idea, go to Section 22.*

32

Watson searches the immaculate sitting room with abject despair.

'You see, but you do not observe.' He mutters.

'What is that?'

'Those were your words to me just before the arrival of the King. So, what am I not observing here? You say Mrs Adler-Norton is involved with a secret society; do they have any signs or rituals that might give them away.'

'Their sigil is an all-seeing eye within a pyramid.'

Watson resumes his search, then cries, 'Holmes, there is a triangular motif on the bell-pull above the fireplace!'

'Excellent, Watson! Give it a tug!'

The doctor complies. Nothing seems to happen but you both here a distinct click from the fireplace.

'Holmes! There is the tiniest triangle on this tile, I think it might be a panel.'

He applies some pressure and the panel slides, revealing a hidden compartment. He returns to you smiling broadly, holding a large photograph of the King and Irene Adler.

The two of you are on your way out of the room when you almost collide with the housekeeper who has brought in a tray of tea. 'Are you alright Father?' she asks in alarm.

'Much improved, thank you. Please convey our gratitude to the lady of the house when she returns,' you say.

Sitting in a cab en route to the Langham to deliver the photograph to the King, you consider the skill, cunning and

audacity of Irene Adler. She made two critical mistakes: the first was falling in love with a man who did not appreciate her worth and the second was marrying a man who loved her so much he was prepared to compromise the secrets of his society to ensure her safety.

You take out the photograph to admire her fine features one last time and ponder whether your victory makes you an agent of Light or Darkness.

THE END

33

'I knew he would send the best, but I must say I find your methodology rather disappointing,' says Irene Adler-Norton.

You ignore the pistol and say with some force, 'I know that you represent an organisation which puts a premium on reason. So, I have come to reason with you.'

You sit up and the barrel of the gun follows you. She waits for you to continue.

'The King is a determined man and, I imagine, a vengeful one when crossed. Subterfuge is your only weapon and your

only defence, and it is now compromised. Your husband was so concerned for your safety that he gave up the secrets of your order, hoping that I could be bought.'

'So, you would betray your promise to him for a King's shilling?'

'A King's ransom, I fancy. His Majesty would give anything to recover the photograph.'

'If I give it up, I certainly have no weapon and no defence, only a vengeful King who takes advice from a cult of medieval zealots.'

'Which is more important, the preservation of your conspiracy or the ruination of the King's conjugal bliss?'

Irene Adler-Norton's eyes blaze and you wonder whether you have pushed her too far. Then she walks to the fireplace, places the gun on the mantel and pulls back a small sliding shutter, revealing a hidden compartment from which she takes a bundle of papers. She hands them to you.

You look at the photograph of the woman and the King. A candid portrait of two lovers, a tinderbox to burn down a dynasty.

Conflicting thoughts trouble your mind, and you avoid Irene Adler-Norton's reproachful gaze as you prepare to leave.

'We will be watching, Mr Holmes.' she says from the doorway.

It was doubtless intended as a dire warning, yet for some unfathomable reason, as you ride to the Langham to see the King, the knowledge excites you.

THE END

34

'This is no religious order. Who are you?' you ask, furious with yourself for losing the initiative.

Squinting, you perceive that you are addressing what appears to be a disembodied mask, the visage of a grotesque demon.

'We are "the Enlightened", or *Illuminati* if you have a preference for Latin.'

You laugh, not attempting to hide your derision, 'A revolutionary movement from the last century?'

'We are still very active, I assure you,' replies the mask, 'the war between light and darkness knows no respite.'

'And who, pray, do you count among the agents of darkness?'

'His Majesty, King Wilhelm of Bohemia for one. He belongs to a religious order known as the Utraquists, another archaic yet sadly very active sect. They wish to return Europe to the Dark Ages.'

'So, you hope to attack the King by scuppering his wedding? It seems rather tawdry.'

'His marriage to the Princess Clotilde would start a powerful dynasty with superstition and tyranny at its heart.'

You hold your tongue and allow the mask to continue its soliloquy.

'We are a force for reason, Mr Holmes, and your coming was foreseen. We would invite you to join us in the fight against ignorance and oppression.'

> ☛ *If you ask where Irene fits into the Illuminati's schemes, go to Section 40.*
>
> ☛ *If you ask why they believe the King is so dangerous, go to Section 45.*

35

The *Illuminati* are wise enough to know that an elaborate initiation would not impress you. Instead, you are presented with a small leatherbound book, it has no title but is embossed with the symbol of the order: an eye enclosed within a pyramid. It appears to be an English translation of a work by **Adam** Weishaupt.

In your journey out of Temple, you peruse the book and learn some of the secrets of the *Illuminati*.

Now that you have agreed to help them, whenever you see the symbol 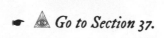 beside an option, it means you can follow a different route to the one given.

Bookmark this section before you proceed. There is a word in this section that also appears on the table in Section 53. Go to the section number on the table instead of the one at the bottom of this page. Try this now. The word in this instance has been highlighted to help you.

☞ 🔺 *Go to Section 37.*

36

'At last King Wilhelm's bloodhound reveals himself. I must say that your infiltration lacks the subtlety and foresight I had expected from London's greatest detective.' says Irene Adler-Norton with a passion that augments her trans-Atlantic vowels.

'You do yourself a disservice madame, I have been expertly outmanoeuvred.'

'Was that flattery? The great Sherlock Holmes would never concede so easily. You met Godfrey, didn't you? Has he convinced you to see the light?'

You nod.

'Oh, this only makes things worse. Your elaborate scheme has brought far too much attention. My people share our proclivity for the theatrical, Mr Holmes, but only as a means of distraction.'

You sit up, remembering that you are not actually wounded. The gun disappears.

After weighing up the situation, you have an idea. 'The King believes you to be motivated by revenge. If you allow his nuptials to proceed unhindered, I will have fulfilled my duties and you will be free to prosecute your war.'

'I think you are making light of a serious situation, Mr Holmes. But you are probably right.'

You leave St John's Wood and make for the Langham Hotel, where the King awaits your news. It is never satisfying to disappoint a client, but your instincts tell you that King Wilhelm of Bohemia is not a good man.

As for Irene Adler-Norton, she was a more-than-worthy adversary, and you wonder whether you will have the pleasure of crossing swords with her again.

THE END

37

No, you took the obvious route. You need to find the code word at your previous location and look it up on the table in Section 53 to find your destination.

☞ *Try again. Return to Section 35.*

38

Defeatedly, you fumble inside your coat for the stolen letters... and then fling them at Irene Adler! Then you dive through the open window, landing ignominiously on the street outside.

Hastening down Serpentine Avenue, the after-image of her gun barrel sends an anxious spasm down your spine until you are well clear of St. John's Wood.

Hours later you are sitting in the comfort of the Langham Hotel nursing an expensive glass of cognac, while the King stares at the photograph and asks you again to recount your exploits.

It was a cheap sleight of hand that secured your victory. Faced with a superior intellect and an expertly wielded firearm, you resorted to throwing a bundle of paper at your opponent before fleeing into the night like a common thief.

His Majesty is ecstatic, but your thoughts are elsewhere. You have bested a worthy adversary and stand to be well-rewarded, but for once in your solitary existence you feel truly alone.

THE END

39

'What am I looking for?' whispers Watson.

'A concealed cupboard or drawer,' you reply, 'the photograph is cabinet sized, too large to be kept on her person, so she must have concealed it somewhere.'

Watson begins a thorough search which he concludes within minutes. 'The room is so uncluttered; how could anything be hidden here?'

You are forced to concur that you might have been mistaken regarding the location of the photograph. There is no hope of searching the other rooms. With no other recourse, you decide to stay put and wait for the lady to return.

☞ *Go to Section 50.*

'There is more to Mrs Norton than a gifted prima donna,' says the voice, with a curious hint of pride, 'the *Illuminati* recruited her during her time at the Imperial Opera, and we have greatly benefited from the influence she holds over her powerful patrons. She was assigned to King Wilhelm, and they developed feelings for one another. We do not discourage such things provided that our interests are not threatened. But then the Knights of the Chalice, an Ultraquist sect, began advising His Majesty.'

'Priests have advised kings for centuries.'

'Come, Mr Holmes, we no longer live in the age of the Borgias, we are three decades on from the Great Exhibition, a time of enlightenment that we have devoted our lives to preserving and furthering.'

'I fail to see how much damage one Bohemian king could do.'

'Then perhaps your vaunted powers of observation have been overstated,' replies the mask sharply, 'Europe is perhaps half a century away from a war that could shake it to its foundations. Even if you cannot fully comprehend the situation Mr Holmes, we would simply ask: where would your loyalties lie?'

It seems you have to make a choice. What will you say?

☞ *State that you will always be on the side of reason? Go to Section 52.*

☞ *Pretend to be sympathetic to the aims of the Illuminati? Go to Section 25.*

☞ *Declare yourself neutral in this absurd war of secret societies? Go to Section 29.*

41

You are given a small leatherbound book, it has no title but is embossed with the symbol of the order: a pyramid containing an eye. It appears to be an English translation of a work by Adam Weishaupt.

On your cab ride out of Temple, you peruse the work and familiarise yourself with the secrets of the *Illuminati*.

In future, when you see the symbol △ beside an option, it means you can follow a different route to the one given, in order to undermine the *Illuminati*'s schemes.

Bookmark this page and go to the table in Section 54. Find your destination on the top row and instead go to the Section directly beneath it.

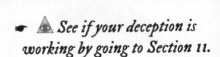

☞ △ *See if your deception is working by going to Section 11.*

42

His Majesty is agitated, pacing up and down his suite at the Langham and fidgeting with the clasp of his cloak.

'Are you absolutely certain?' he asks for the fifth time.

'That your wedding can proceed unhindered, yes, Your Majesty.'

Finally accepting the news, the King exhales a long-held breath of relief, smiles broadly, and removes one of his rings, a thick band of pure gold, housing a ruby of breath-taking size. He is clearly about to offer it to you. This is too much.

'Please, Your Majesty. My expenses have been more than sufficient, no further payment is necessary.'

He places a large, regal hand on your shoulder. 'I am in your debt Mr Holmes. You have rendered me a great service.'

You stiffen at this undeserved adulation. Such a man might be as unworthy of your sympathy as he is of Irene Adler, but you have, nevertheless, betrayed your client and possibly altered the course of European history.

THE END

43

'I think not,' you reply.

Gathering up the letters and photograph, you prepare to leave.

'Mr Holmes, you should know that there is more to this affair than a spurned lover's revenge.'

'You are referring, I believe, to a group of conspirators who refer to themselves as "the Enlightened"?'

It is difficult not to derive some pleasure from her astonishment.

'You would be well-advised not to cross them,' she says softly.

You deliver your parting shot with relish: 'They - *you* - have nothing to fear. Your secrets are perfectly safe with me.'

You leave St. John's Wood for the Langham, where King Wilhelm greets you cordially and invites you to dine in his private room.

'Your reputation is well-deserved, Sherlock Holmes!' he says, staring incredulously at the photograph.

You permit yourself to bask in the King's adulation, take a carefree sip of your cognac and - 'Ack! Ack! Ack!' - discover it has been laced with pepper!

His Majesty's reddening visage indicates that his drink has been similarly corrupted. Tears pour from his eyes as he gropes for a napkin.

You consult your memory and recall the briefest glimpse of the youthful waiter who served you. Fine, one might say feminine, features with dark, intelligent eyes and the enigmatic smile of a worthy opponent.

'Where is the photograph?' chokes the King when he has recovered his wits.

You hold the cognac up to the light and wonder how best to inform His Majesty that recovering the same object twice will require additional expenses.

THE END

44

You move to the fireplace and slide back the panel of the secret compartment. It contains a photograph and a sheaf of letters.

'Here! What do you think you're doing?' shouts the frustratingly astute housekeeper.

Irene Adler-Norton utters a shocked, 'Father?' But there is something akin to amusement in her gaze that tells you that your disguise has failed. She turns to her housekeeper, 'Could you leave us for a moment Mrs Bridges?'

The sharp-eyed servant opens her mouth to object, changes her mind and leaves the room.

'Mr Sherlock Holmes, I believe?'

'You are well-informed madame,' you reply, rather lamely.

'I knew the King would purchase the very best.'

The quasi-compliment affects you more strongly than you would have expected. 'We appear to be at an impasse,' is your reply.

'Indeed. Would you allow me to propose a way to break it? One that will ensure no one comes to any harm?'

You nod.

'You know, of course, that I was furious with Wilhelm when he abandoned me, and the photograph presented me with the means to return the pain he had caused.'

'Indeed.'

'You also know that I am now married, to a good man, with whom I have every intention of loving for the rest of my life. The contents of the photograph would be as disastrous to my future happiness as they would be to the King's if they became public.'

She moves towards you and takes the papers from your hand; she is close enough that you can fully appreciate the intelligence and mystery of her dark eyes. 'Mr Holmes, I wonder if you might convey the details of this impasse to the King, put his mind at rest and, in doing so, allow me to live out my days in peace?'

☞ *Do you agree to her terms? If so, go to Section 24.*

☞ *Or would you rather retrieve the papers and return to the King? Then go to Section 43.*

45

'There was nothing exceptional about King Wilhelm. Like most aristocrats he was content to spend his time carousing, hunting and duelling until he came under the influence of the Knights of the Chalice, an Ultraquist sect bent on returning Europe to an early form of Christianity, one where terror and cruelty are liberally applied to keep everyone in their place.'

'It seems unlikely that people will choose to return to the Dark Ages in a time of progressive thought and scientific advancement,' you say.

'You are correct. Such regression requires an apocalyptic catalyst such as war, famine, plague, or all three together. The Knights of the Chalice think of the world as their chess board with people as pawns and calamity as their pieces. Civilisation is like a candle in a hurricane, Mr Holmes. Will you help us preserve the light?'

What will you do?

- Help the Illuminati and hope you are on the right side of history? Go to Section 52.

- Pretend to help the Illuminati but remain loyal to your client? Go to Section 25.

- Declare yourself neutral? This sounds like a fantasy. Go to Section 29.

46

'Where could it be?' asks Watson, 'the room is so tidy and there are no obvious nooks.'

'There are symbols of their organisation, look for anything that resembles a pyramid or an eye.'

Watson scours the room then cries, 'Holmes, the bellpull above the fireplace!'

You commend his powers of observation. The bellpull has an embroidered triangular pattern that might well be interpreted as a pyramid.

Watson makes to tug the bellpull but waits for your approval. You nod.

You hear the faintest of clicks and Watson locates the source, pulling back a panel reveals a hidden compartment in the fireplace.

Watson gasps, 'They're all here, Holmes. The photograph and the letters.

'Excellent Watson. Now return them to their hiding place if you please and leave the panel just slightly ajar.'

The doctor stares at you incredulously. 'I do not understand.'

'We must let the King know that we have found his photograph.'

☞ *Head back to Baker Street in Section 4.*

47

You move to the fireplace and activate the secret compartment; it contains a photograph and a sheaf of letters. As you swiftly transfer them to the pocket stitched inside your clergyman's disguise, you hear the unmistakable sound of a service pistol being cocked.

Slowly turning around, you come face-to-face with the muzzle of the firearm, held unwaveringly by Mrs Irene Adler-Norton.

'Those belong to me, Mr Sherlock Holmes,' she says firmly, but without a trace of menace.

'You are in the process of blackmailing a member of the European aristocracy, do you wish to add common murder to your list of accomplishments?' you ask.

'There is nothing common about you, Mr Holmes,' she smiles, 'but if you had used your fabled investigative talents, you would have discovered that the *Illuminati* are both implacable friends and deadly enemies.'

She is not bluffing, there is more at stake here than a spurned lover's revenge.

Think quickly, is this the time for ...

☞ *Talk? Go to Section 49.*

☞ *Action? Go to Section 38.*

48

'You are in the employ of King Wilhelm of Bohemia, are you not?' She seems well-apprised of the situation and takes your silence as confirmation.

In view of the deftly wielded weapon, you choose your words with care: 'His Majesty believes there is something in your possession that could endanger his future felicity.'

'It is no longer in my possession. The photograph is being held in a vault with instructions that it is to be released to the wider world in the event of my death or disappearance.'

'Why not simply return or destroy the photograph?'

'Monarchs are not renowned for their clemency; I feel much safer with this collateral.'

'Then you have no intention of using it against him, if you are left in peace?'

'None. I have found happiness with a better man. My own lust for vengeance is quelled.'

You nod. 'May I convey this information to His Majesty?'

'Please do.' She lowers the pistol and allows you and Watson to leave.

'What a remarkable woman,' exclaims Watson, finally breaking the silence in the cab as it makes its way to the Langham.

'Indeed,' you muse, 'indeed.'

THE END

49

'How do you propose to resolve this impasse?' you ask.

'First return my property, then return to the King and convince him that the photograph and letters were destroyed in the fire that broke out here this afternoon.'

'Even if his majesty believed me, do you still intend to use them against him.'

'Yes.'

You remain completely still.

'Come, Mr Holmes - death before dishonour? I give you my word that they will not be made public before his wedding to the Scandinavian princess.'

'And then?'

'They still give us considerable influence. Rumours will reach the King that the photograph was recovered. I must confess that my original plan lacked the subtlety of an Illuminatus, I must thank you for showing me my error.'

You retrieve the papers and place them in the hidden compartment, then leave without another word.

☞ *Return to the King at Section 42.*

50

You maintain your feigned convalescence. Watson takes a seat beside the window and watches as your street theatre disperses. A serving girl brings you tea.

A full hour goes by before you here the sound of an elegant landau pulling up outside, followed by the door being opened and the housekeeper explaining your presence.

The sitting room door is opened, and a beautiful young woman enters. You make a gallant attempt to stand but are overcome with affected dizziness. Watson rises politely then resumes his seat at a nod from the lady.

She smiles sympathetically, dismissing the worried housekeeper, 'thank you Mrs Bridges.'

Just as you start to believe your deception successful, Irene Adler-Norton says:

'The famous Sherlock Holmes and his companion Doctor John Watson.'

Watson gets to his feet again, but she is faster. A small pistol has appeared in her unwavering hand, and it is pointed directly at your head.

☞ ⚠ *Perhaps you had better explain yourself by going to Section 48.*

You read the letter aloud:

My Dear Mr. Sherlock Holmes,

— You really did it very well. I had been warned against you months ago. I had been told that, if the King employed an agent, it would certainly be you. And your address had been given me. Yet, with all this, you made me reveal what you wanted to know. Even after I became suspicious, I found it hard to think evil of such a dear, kind old clergyman. But, you know, I have been trained as an actress myself. Male costume is nothing new to me. I often take advantage of the freedom which it gives.

Godfrey and I both thought the best resource was flight, when pursued by so formidable an antagonist; so you will find the nest empty when you call to-morrow. As to the photograph, your client may rest in peace. I love and am loved by a better man than he. The King may do what he will without hindrance from one whom he has cruelly wronged. I keep it only to safeguard myself, and to preserve a weapon which will always secure me from any steps which he might take in the future. I leave a photograph which he might care to possess; and I remain, dear Mr. Sherlock Holmes,

Very truly yours,

Irene Norton, née Adler.

The King breathes a sigh, 'Oh what a Queen she would have made, is it not a pity that she was not on my level?'

'She is indeed on a very different level to Your Majesty,' you mutter, 'I am sorry that I have not been able to bring this business to a more successful conclusion.'

'On the contrary, my dear sir, nothing could be more successful. I know that her word is inviolate. The photograph is now as safe as if it were in the fire. Please name your price!'

You could ask for anything. But you ask the King for just one thing: the photograph of the woman who bested you.

THE END

52

'I will help you,' you promise.

'That is good,' says the Illuminatus with unalloyed relief and starts to remove the mask.

Just before his face is revealed, you cannot resist: 'Mr Godfrey Norton, I presume?'

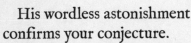

His wordless astonishment confirms your conjecture.

'You are, no doubt, wondering whether I inculcated Irene? Quite the contrary, she recruited me after the King threw her away. I was already impressed with the writing of Adam Weishaupt but never dared to dream his organisation still flourished.'

'You are revealing quite a lot for a member of a secret order,' you comment dryly.

'We know quite a lot about you, Mr Holmes. You will be a great asset to the *Illuminati*, but we are well aware that we cannot hope to retain your services by attempting to hide things from you.'

'And what services do you require?'

'You must proceed as if this meeting never happened. The King must not be alerted, and Irene must behave as if you were still her adversary. You will attempt to retrieve the letters and the photograph; you will fail but all parties will be satisfied.'

☞ *If you think their request sounds reasonable, go to Section 35.*

☞ *If you think the Illuminati sound like a lunatic cult that must be stopped, go to Section 41.*

Codeword	Go to	Codeword	Go to
CUDGEL	Section 30	ADAM	Section 16
ULSTER	Section 26	WEDGE	Section 46
LOST	Section 13	BRIDGES	Section 36

Section 44	Section 19	Section 51	Section 11	Section 39	Section 48
Section 47	Section 12	Section 21	Section 3	Section 32	Section 33

THE
NAVAL TREATY

1

There is an ingenious kind of paper, infused with an extract of lichen, which turns red under acidic conditions. It is named after an Old Norse word meaning 'moss dye'.

One July morning you are about to employ this litmus paper in a critical experiment when you note the arrival of your colleague.

'You come at a crisis, Watson,' you warn. 'If this paper remains blue, all is well. If it turns red, it means a man's life.'

Dipping the paper into a test tube confirms your suspicions - a deep crimson, the colour of murder.

You signal for Watson to help himself to pipe tobacco while you hastily write up your grim findings. There is an agitation in the good doctor's demeanour that arouses your curiosity.

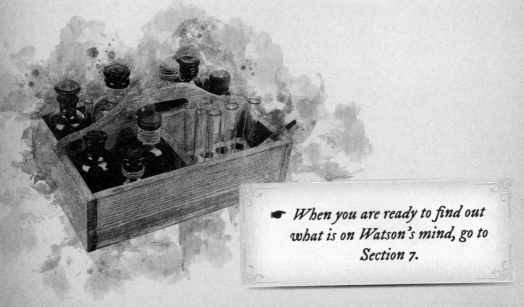

☞ *When you are ready to find out what is on Watson's mind, go to Section 7.*

2

'Ah, you suspect me of being a foreigner - a French spy perhaps?' Charles Gorot laughs.

You say nothing and allow him to elaborate.

'My family are, indeed, of French extraction - Huguenot to be precise. My Calvinist forefathers were forced to flee Catholic persecution and took refuge in England. So, you see, I have no ancestral loyalty to France.'

Watson clarifies, 'The official persecution of Protestants ended over a century ago.'

Gorot concedes, adding, 'But the prejudice continues, or so I am told.'

☞ *You thank Charles Gorot for his time, and decide it is time to meet Percy Phelps. Go to Section 40.*

3

Joseph Harrison hands Percy Phelps a glass of water and he drinks deeply before submitting to your questions.

You begin by asking, 'Can you describe the intruder?'

'I could see little of him,' Percy replies, 'for he was gone like a flash. He was wrapped in some sort of cloak, which came across the lower part of his face. One thing only I am sure of, and that is that he had some weapon in his hand. It looked to me like a long knife. I distinctly saw the gleam of it as he turned to run.'

Percy Phelps is clearly shaken by the experience. 'I believe that I am the unconscious centre of some monstrous conspiracy and that my life is aimed at, as well as my honour.'

'What did you do after the intruder fled?' you ask.

'I should have followed him through the open window if I had been stronger. As it was, I rang the bell and roused the house. It took me some little time, for the bell rings in the kitchen and the servants all sleep upstairs, so I shouted and that brought Joseph down, and he roused the others. Joseph and the groom found marks on the bed outside the window but the weather has been so dry lately that they found it hopeless to follow the trail across the grass. There's a place, however, on the wooden fence that skirts the road, which shows signs, they tell me, as if someone had got over and had snapped the top of the rail in doing so. I have said nothing to the local police yet, for I thought I had best have your opinion first.'

> ☞ *There is no time to lose;*
> *you must wrap up this case.*
> *Go to Section 21.*

4

On the night the treaty was stolen, Phelps went down to see the commissionaire and heard the bell coming from his own room.

You know that Joseph was in London that night and it is curious that he did not arrange to travel back with his future brother-in-law.

What if Joseph had visited Percy's workplace that evening, entered the office through the side entrance, found it empty and rang the commissionaire to announce his arrival. But then seeing the treaty and recognising its value, he pocketed it and fled back to Woking.

How will you proceed?

☛ *Accuse him then and there before he gets wind of your suspicions? Go to Section 49.*

☛ *Construct an elaborate trap? Go to Section 45.*

5

Joseph Harrison flushes irritably. He is clearly not accustomed to being questioned so directly.

'I am not a broker, Mr Holmes. If you need financial guidance, I recommend you seek the advice of a professional - for all the good they are.'

Perhaps your question was indelicate but it has evidently touched a nerve. Mr Harrison's joviality is a veneer that conceals considerable frustration.

☞ *Not wishing to vex him further, you ask to see your client. Follow Joseph to Section 28.*

6

The content of the letter is vague. However, your knowledge of graphology tells you that it was written by a very determined *woman*. You bring this to Watson's attention but he can offer no suggestion as to who it might be.

'Have you shown the letter to anyone else?' you ask.

'Only to Mary.'

'And what is your wife's judgement?'

'She was certain that the letter would be of interest to you and insisted that I waste no time in bringing it to your attention.'

'Her instincts are infallible.'

Watson is clearly delighted to have piqued your curiosity and is eager to depart in search of answers.

☛ *Will you take the case and the earliest available train to Woking? If so, hasten to Section 25.*

☛ *Or do you favour a more cautious approach? Then saunter over to Section 9.*

7

Watson hands you a letter. The sender's address is Briarbrae, Woking and it reads:

My dear Watson,

I have no doubt that you can remember 'Tadpole' Phelps, who was in the fifth form when you were in the third. It is possible, even, that you may have heard that, through my uncle's influence, I obtained a good appointment at the Foreign Office, and that I was in a situation of trust and honour until a horrible misfortune came suddenly to blast my career.

There is no use writing of the details of that dreadful event. In the event of your acceding to my request, it is probable that I shall have to narrate them to you. I have only just recovered from nine weeks of brain-fever and am still exceedingly weak.

Do you think that you could bring your friend Mr Holmes down to see me? I should like to have his opinion of the case, though the authorities assure me that nothing more can be done. Do try to bring him down, and as soon as possible. Every minute seems an hour while I live in this state of horrible suspense. Assure him that if I have not asked his advice sooner, it is not because I do not appreciate his talents but because I have been off my head ever since the blow fell.

Now I am clear again, though I dare not think of it too much for fear of a relapse. I am still so weak that I have to write, as you see, by dictating. Do try to bring him.

Your old school fellow,

Percy Phelps

☞ When you have the gist, go to Section 6.

8

He had been trading in stocks but apparently not very successfully. In fact, it is likely that he was a victim of the recent stock-market panic, which left many bankrupt.

The treaty is still in his possession, right under your nose. By inviting you to Briarbrae, Percy Phelps has undoubtably expedited the thief's desire to be rid of his prize.

How will you proceed?

☛ *Accuse him then and there before he gets wind of your suspicions? Go to Section 49.*

☛ *Construct an elaborate trap? Go to Section 45.*

9

Watson cannot hide his exasperation as you take a seat and light your pipe. However, you refuse to be hastened when there are questions to be answered.

'Tell me about your friend Phelps, Watson.'

'He is the nephew of Lord Holdhurst.'

'The Conservative politician?'

'Yes, and Foreign Minister. The relationship earned Percy a hard time at school. But he was a brilliant scholar and went on to Cambridge and thence to join his uncle at the Foreign Office.'

'How would you describe his character?'

'It has been a while since we last corresponded. We were little more than boys.'

'Give me a child until he is seven ...' you say.

Watson smiles, unwilling to argue with Aristotle.

'Did "Tadpole" Phelps lack mental stamina?' you ask.

'He was a nervous, sensitive boy. Yet he bore our constant taunts with admirable fortitude.'

'And you have no inkling as to what caused the scholarly Phelps such anxiety that he needed another to write his entreaty?'

'None at all.'

You cannot deny that the letter has aroused your interest. But would it be more prudent to begin your investigation here in London or to visit Phelps in Woking?

- ☞ *If you think there are answers here in the city, go to Section 29.*

- ☞ *If you think that Surrey would be a better place to make enquiries, go to Section 25.*

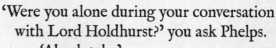

10

'Were you alone during your conversation with Lord Holdhurst?' you ask Phelps.
'Absolutely.'
'Could you have been overheard?'
'The Foreign Minister's room is large and we stood in its centre. It was about 30 feet each way.'
'And you were speaking low?'
'My uncle's voice is always remarkably low. I hardly spoke at all.'
'Regarding the document, who would benefit from discovering its contents?'
'It defined the position of Great Britain towards the Triple Alliance. The French or Russian Embassy would pay handsomely for such information.'
'Do you know anything of the commissionaire?'
'Nothing except that he is an old soldier.'
'What regiment?'
'The Coldstream Guards.'
'And his wife?'
'I know even less. A bellicose woman - she often smells of gin.'
Your rapid interrogation is causing Phelps some distress and Miss Harrison looks at you admonishingly.

☛ *You decide to return to London to continue the investigation.*
Go to Section 14.

11

You head over to Scotland Yard and introduce yourself to Mr Forbes, a small, foxy man with a rather hostile demeanour.

Explaining that you have been briefed on the case of the missing naval treaty by the Foreign Minister, you offer whatever assistance you can give.

Forbes begrudgingly accepts your help and you exchange notes. He has reached a number of dead ends with his suspects but there is one thing in particular that vexes him.

'Apparently, Mr Phelps rang the commissionaire's bell and it was his wife, Mrs Tangey, who answered. Phelps asked for a cup of coffee but, when some time had passed, he left his desk to investigate the delay. He found Mr Tangey asleep with the kettle boiling over and no sign of the missus. Then the bell from Phelps' room rang again. The two men rushed upstairs to find the room empty and the treaty missing. Why would a thief announce his presence by ringing a bell, Mr Holmes?'

☞ *You decide it is time to visit your client in Woking. Go to Section 40.*

12

The train from Woking returns you to London, where you believe you will find both the treaty and its thief. You think it likely that whoever took it was in some way connected with the Foreign Office.

You take a hansom from Waterloo to Scotland Yard and meet Mr Forbes, who is visibly delighted at the prospect of an end to this mystery. A variety of means and motives present themselves but you have four possible suspects.

Which of the following has convinced you of their guilt?

☛ *If you suspect Lord Holdhurst, go to Section 20.*

☛ *If you believe Mr Tangey (or his wife) is responsible, go to Section 32.*

☛ *If you think Percy's colleague, Charles Gorot, took the treaty, go to Section 47.*

13

What was the thief's motive for taking the treaty? Was it simply a crime of opportunity, motivated by a need for money or an act of revenge based on a bitter jealousy? Did he watch Percy's declining health with a sense of regret, cold indifference, or jubilation?

☞ *If you think it was a question of money, go to Section 8.*

☞ *If you believe revenge was the underlying motive, go to Section 22.*

14

Joseph Harrison drives you to Woking Station and you are soon on a train bound for London.

Watson assures you that his medical practice will not require his presence for the next couple of days and he is most eager to accompany you. You discuss the unfortunate Phelps and have both been equally impressed by his fiancée; somewhat less so by her unctuous brother.

Your train pulls into Waterloo at 3.20 p.m. and, after a hasty buffet luncheon, you take a cab to Scotland Yard, where you meet Mr Forbes, the detective in charge of the case. He is a small, sharp-featured man and not terribly experienced. Nevertheless, he quickly attempts to assert his authority.

'I've heard of your methods before now, Mr Holmes. You are ready enough to use all the information that the police can lay at your disposal and then you try to finish the case yourself and bring discredit on them.'

You have no time for this.

'On the contrary,' you reply. 'Out of my last fifty-three cases, my name has only appeared in four. The police have taken all the credit in forty-nine. I don't blame you for not knowing this, for you are young and inexperienced, but if you wish to get on in your new duties, you will work with me and not against me.'

That takes the wind out of his sails.

'I'd be very glad of a hint or two,' he says dejectedly. 'I've certainly had no credit from the case so far.'

Having established that you are in charge, how will you proceed?

Mr Forbes

☛ *If you would like to discuss Phelps's colleague, Charles Gorot, go to Section 19.*

☛ *If you are interested in Mr Tangey and his wife, go to Section 34.*

☛ *If you would like to visit Lord Holdhurst, go to Section 46.*

15

At Scotland Yard you meet Inspector Lestrade, from whom you learn that Percy Phelps had reported the theft of an important document from the Foreign Office.

You are introduced to Mr Forbes, the detective in charge of the investigation - a small man with sharp eyes and a far-from-friendly manner.

'I've heard of you, Mr Holmes. Have you come to make use of our intelligence so you can finish the case and elevate yourself at our expense?'

'Nothing could be further from the truth, Mr Forbes,' you reply. 'I have every confidence that the Yard can conclude this affair without my interference but, if I can be of any assistance, I am at your disposal.'

Forbes mulls this over and his expression softens somewhat.

'To be honest, we're at a dead end. If you could provide a new perspective, there would be no objection.'

'What do you know of the missing document?'

'Very little. The Foreign Office have been reluctant to discuss its contents, other than that it pertains to a matter of national importance.'

'And the circumstances of its disappearance?'

'Apparently on 23 May, Mr Phelps stayed late to make a copy of the document at the behest of Lord Holdhurst. He left it unguarded on his desk in order to find the commissionaire and, when he returned, it had gone.'

Reading Forbes's dejected aspect, you conclude that he had some credible suspects but has been unable to obtain corroborating evidence. You ask him about them.

'There was a colleague of Mr Phelps's by the name of Charles Gorot who had been working late on the night of the theft,' he recalls. 'But he retired before Mr Phelps started work on the document.

'Then there was the commissionaire's wife, Mrs Tangey. She hurried from the office after the time of the theft. We questioned her at her home and conducted a thorough search the very same evening. But we found nothing.'

You have time to follow up on one of these suspects if you wish to meet with your client tomorrow. Who would you like to investigate?

Mr Forbes

☞ *If you would like to visit Mr and Mrs Tangey, go to Section 37.*

☞ *If you would prefer to see Charles Gorot, go to Section 18.*

16

He must have visited Percy on the night of the theft and found the clerks' room empty with the treaty lying in plain view. Even to an uneducated brute, its value would have been obvious.

It was an act of audacious opportunism and, with no clear plan as to what to do with the precious document, he has kept it here all this time.

How will you proceed?

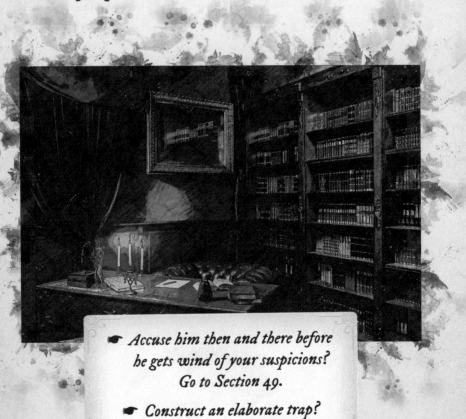

☞ *Accuse him then and there before he gets wind of your suspicions?*
Go to Section 49.

☞ *Construct an elaborate trap?*
Go to Section 45.

17

'Did you tell anyone other than Mr Phelps that you intended to have the treaty copied?' you ask.

'I did not,' replies Holdhurst.

'Does anyone share his room?'

'A handful of clerks. Charles Gorot was the only one working late on the night of the theft. He went home before my nephew commenced work on the copy and has satisfied the police regarding his whereabouts.'

'And the commissionaire, has he been questioned?'

'Mr Tangey and his wife were questioned by Mr Forbes of Scotland Yard. My nephew accompanied the detective to their residence on the night of the theft and a thorough search was carried out. The Tangeys were the most obvious suspects but the police could find nothing to incriminate them.'

'Who would benefit from being privy to the contents of the treaty?'

'The French and Russian embassies would undoubtedly pay well for such a document.'

'And if this were to happen?'

'It would be a catastrophe.'

'The fact that no such catastrophe has occurred suggests that it is not yet in their possession.'

'True. Perhaps the thief is negotiating a price.'

☞ *If you would like to visit Mr Forbes, go to Section 11.*

☞ *If you decide it is time to visit the client in Woking, go to Section 40.*

18

'We've been shadowing Mr Gorot these past nine weeks and turned up nothing,' Forbes grumbles. 'He'll be at the Foreign Office now.'

Excellent! You can question the suspect and view the scene of the crime. You travel with Forbes to the Foreign Office and summon a slightly perplexed Charles Gorot.

He is a smartly attired young man with a pleasantly relaxed demeanour. You conclude that he is not the victim of any financial deprivation.

Gorot shakes your hand energetically. 'I have heard of you, Mr Holmes. Is this about Percy's treaty again? The detectives have already asked innumerable questions and made a thorough search of my residence.'

Charles Gorot

'Could you think of anyone who would benefit from the acquisition of the treaty?' you ask.

'Anyone looking to make themselves wealthy, I should think. Any of the Empire's enemies would pay handsomely for such a document.'

'Enough for a junior diplomat to retire comfortably?'

Charles Gorot smiles. 'I already consider myself very comfortable and very fortunate. My family invested wisely, unlike the poor souls who have seen their stocks reduced to worthless paper in the latest panic.'

'Can you recall your movements on the night the treaty was taken?' you ask.

'Certainly. I worked into the evening. Percy went out to dinner and I left before he returned.'

'Does he have many social connections here?'

'Not really. I suppose being the Minister's nephew puts him at a disadvantage.'

'What about visitors?'

'His fiancée's brother has a broker nearby and they take the train together when he is in town.'

Gorot is answering your haphazard questions with commendable calm.

'What is your impression of Mr Phelps?'

He pauses to think.

'In truth, I can't say that I know Percy very well at all.'

☞ If you ask Charles Gorot about his surname, go to Section 2.

☞ If you decide it is time to visit the client in Woking, go to Section 40.

19

You ask Forbes about Percy Phelps's colleague, Charles Gorot.

'He seemed a possible suspect, what with his French name and all, but we had him followed and turned up nothing.'

'You suspected connections with France?'

'Yes but it turns out that his family is Hugh ... Huge ...'

'Huguenot?' Watson interjects helpfully. 'Protestant exiles.'

'Yes. Apparently, they're still unpopular over there so we had no reason to suspect him of being a spy.'

'And he can account for his movements after leaving the office?'

'Yes. His version of events has been verified. The policeman on duty that night saw him leave.'

☛ *If you decide to ask Forbes about Mr and Mrs Tangey, go to Section 34.*

☛ *If you want to return to Woking immediately, go to Section 39.*

20

Mr Forbes is beyond incredulous when you propose that Lord Holdhurst stole the treaty. 'What possible reason could the future Prime Minister have for stealing his own documents?'

You suggest that he is having financial difficulties, as evinced by his re-soled shoes.

'Most of the British aristocracy have to make do and mend these days!' counters Forbes. 'Mr Holmes, are you actually suggesting that a peer of the realm would betray his own country because he couldn't afford new shoes?'

There is considerable hostility in the room. Even Watson is shaking his head in disbelief. Forbes reluctantly writes up your conclusions and you make your way back to Baker Street in silence.

The following day you receive a curt note from your brother Mycroft: '*You will be fortunate to find work as a consultant chimney sweep after this debacle.*'

You light your pipe and enter a mood of dark introspection, vowing to avoid affairs of State in future.

THE END

21

You are certain that the thief is someone you have encountered during your investigations. The problem lies in the surplus of evidence but you do not have the luxury of time; any delay will allow the thief to make their escape.

First you must narrow down your suspects.

☞ *Do you think the thief is a resident of Briarbrae? If so, go to Section 26.*

☞ *Or do you believe the culprit is in London? Then go to Section 12.*

22

You return to London, convinced that the treaty has been secreted somewhere at the Foreign Office.

Lord Holdhurst is displeased at your arrival and the investigation is impeded because not even the police are permitted to rifle through state secrets.

After a day of scant progress, you hear from Briarbrae that there has been another break-in. Fortunately, Joseph had moved back into his old bedchamber and surprised the intruder.

A week passes and then disaster! The Russian Embassy has acquired the treaty and the country is on the brink of war.

You have been outmanoeuvred. Perhaps by a foreign agent or perhaps by an enemy closer to home. In any case, it is unlikely that Her Majesty's Government will be calling on your services in future.

THE END

23

'Do you reside here at Briarbrae, Mr Harrison?'
you ask.

'I do. I've had a room here since Percy's
misfortune. I'm able to help out and keep my
sister company while she cares for him.'

'And you are able to make a living here as a helpmeet?'

Harrison bridles slightly but the impish grin quickly returns.

'I make my way. I dabble in stocks and shares, which grants me
a certain independence. Besides, I'm happy to forgo advancing my
own interests while Annie and Percy have need of me.'

'You must excuse my directness, Mr Harrison, but any snippet of
information, no matter how trivial, could prove vital.'

'What would you like to know, Mr Holmes?'

'Your sister is to marry Mr Phelps. How did this come about?'

'Percy was travelling in Northumberland last winter when he met
my sister. We came down to Woking together and I stayed on when
Percy fell ill.'

'It seems an advantageous match. For your sister.'

You are testing Mr Harrison's jovial veneer and, for a moment, it
almost seems to crack.

'Our father was an ironmaster and Percy's uncle could
conceivably be the next Prime Minister. Yes, Mr Holmes, it is an
advantageous connection. Are you of the opinion that someone
like Annie, for all her
good qualities, should
"know her place"?'

*You sense that the
atmosphere has
become considerably
less cordial.*

☞ *Do you want to ask Joseph about his
investments? If so, go to Section 5.*

☞ *Or perhaps you should soften your
tone and enquire about Percy, in
which case go to Section 28.*

24

Percy Phelps is arrested on a charge of treason and Lord Holdsworth is unable to keep the case out of the papers. Your brother Mycroft advises you to stay clear of Whitehall, where you are now persona non grata.

Three days before the date of his trial, you learn that Percy has taken his own life.

Many are convinced that this proves his guilt but you are not so sure. There is something you missed and your oversight has cost an innocent man his life.

THE END

25

You take the early train from Waterloo and arrive at Woking in under an hour. After a pleasant stroll through the Surrey countryside, you come at last to Briarbrae, which reveals itself to be a large, detached house with extensive grounds.

The housekeeper takes your cards and shows you both to the drawing room. A moment later you are joined by a heavy-set man in his mid-thirties. He has a ruddy complexion and a merry demeanour.

The man shakes your hands energetically. 'I'm so glad you have come,' he effuses. 'Percy has been beside himself, as have his

Joseph Harrison

mother and father. They asked me to come in their stead because the subject causes them such distress.'

The man is wearing a single-breasted waistcoat with a gold locket that bears the monogram 'J.H.'

'We still have to apprise ourselves of the details,' you say. 'I perceive that you are not, yourself, a member of the family.'

The man is taken aback, then looks down at his locket and laughs heartily. 'Joseph Harrison is my name. My sister Annie is Percy's fiancée, so I shall be one of the family before too long.'

Joseph Harrison shifts awkwardly under your scrutiny but he remains cheerful. 'Would you follow me, gentlemen? I shall take you to see Percy.'

☞ *Would you like to delay your interview and talk to Joseph Harrison? If so, go to Section 23.*

☞ *If you would rather see the client first and discover the nature of this case, hasten to Section 28.*

26

The recent attempted burglary has convinced you that the thief, and possibly the treaty, are here in Briarbrae. Have you enough evidence to decide which of the residents took the document?

☛ *If you suspect Percy Phelps took the treaty himself, go to Section 41.*

☛ *If you believe Percy's fiancée Annie has the treaty, go to Section 53.*

☛ *If you think Annie's brother Joseph is the thief, go to Section 35.*

27

'You did not sleep in this room before your convalescence, is that correct?'

'Yes. It was not originally a bed-chamber but, when Joseph arrived, we had it refurbished for his use ...' Phelps' eyes widen. 'You don't think that he ...?'

'Where is Mr Harrison now?' you enquire.

'He said he had urgent business in town and left just before the police arrived.'

You turn to the detectives. 'Forgive me, gentlemen. I regret I have provided you with the correct address but the wrong resident. Mr Phelps, if you would be so kind as to furnish the constables with a complete description of your future brother-in-law. I fear he may be far from here by now.'

You look at the scroll of grey paper in your hand.

'Come, Watson. We must away to the Foreign Office with all haste.'

You admonish yourself for missing an obvious clue and causing your client unnecessary distress, but you pledge to restore his esteem in the eyes of his uncle when you return the naval treaty to its proper place.

THE END

28

You are shown to a ground-floor sitting room, which has been refurnished as a convalescent's bedchamber. Floral arrangements have been added everywhere to create a more cheerful ambiance. The window is open, allowing the rich scent of summer to fill the room.

On a sofa near to the window lies a young man. He is very pale and clearly ravaged by anxiety.

A woman with thick black hair and dark eyes rises from her seat beside him. She appears to be about to leave but the young man clings to her hand. Joseph sweeps the room with his cheery smile and leaves discreetly.

'Watson!' The pale man's frown becomes a pained smile. 'And this must be your celebrated friend, Sherlock Holmes?'

You watch the two old school friends exchange pleasantries and note the expression of the young woman - there is concern and forlorn hope written on her fine features.

At length Percy turns to you and addresses the matter in hand.

'On 23 May, my uncle, Lord Holdhurst, called me into his private room and gave me a commission. He handed me a document that he explained was a secret treaty between England and Italy. Such a thing would not ordinarily leave his office but he urgently required a copy. I was to wait until everyone else had left, make the copy and immediately return the documents to his safe.

'I waited until the other clerks had retired but my colleague, Charles Gorot, was working late so I went out to dine. When I returned, I was alone. The document was very long and in French. By nine o'clock I had only completed a third of it and I realised I would not be able take my intended train home. I started to feel sleepy so I rang the bell for some coffee and was surprised when the commissionaire's wife, Mrs Tangey, answered the call.

'When, after some time, the coffee failed to arrive, I went down

Percy Phelps

to the commissionnaire's office and found Mr Tangey asleep and the kettle boiling over. There was no sign of Mrs Tangey.

'Suddenly a bell rang, waking Mr Tangey, and I was alarmed to see that it came from my own room. Tangey and I hastened upstairs to find the room empty and the treaty gone.'

Percy Phelps's breathing becomes more rapid as anxiety takes hold. Annie clasps his hand and you wait for the panic to subside before you ask: 'How many entrances are there to the room in which you work?'

'Two. If the thief had used the front entrance, we would have crossed paths, so they must have used the side door. The only person seen leaving by the side entrance was Mrs Tangey. I notified Scotland Yard and we visited her abode that same night. The police questioned the Tangeys and searched their home and there was no sign of the treaty. Finally, in despair, I took the late train back to Woking.'

☛ *If you ask Phelps to go back over the events leading to the theft, go to Section 10.*

☛ *If you let him continue his narrative, go to Section 52.*

29

Where should you start? You do not yet know the cause of Percy Phelps's distress but perhaps an oblique approach will prove a faster path to the truth.

You could consult the police to determine whether Phelps is the subject of an ongoing investigation. Bear in mind that your relationship with Scotland Yard is ambivalent; its detectives have a grudging admiration for your methods but do not enjoy being relegated to the margins of a case.

Or perhaps you could go to the seat of government and learn something about your client and his employer. Affairs of State are the ambit of your brother Mycroft so it would be prudent to consult him first. However, you are generally reluctant to seek his counsel unless the case merits it.

☛ *If you decide to talk to the police, go to Section 15.*

☛ *If you arrange a meeting with your brother, go to Section 55.*

30

You are certain that Phelps' distress is genuine. It is obvious that he lacks the ruthlessness for such an audacious crime.

'Wait!' you command.

The officers pause at the doorway as Phelps sobs piteously.

You ignore the bewildered stares and marshal your thoughts. Someone tried to break into Percy's room - someone close to him - who knew that the treaty was here all along.

Who betrayed Percy's trust?

☞ *Was it his fiancée, Annie Harrison? If you think so, go to Section 31.*

☞ *If you suspect her brother Joseph, go to Section 27.*

31

Did Percy really dictate the letter or was it part of a carefully conceived plot to send you down the wrong path?

From the moment you scrutinized her handwriting, you knew that Annie Harrison was a formidable woman but you assumed such fortitude came from a noble heart. It seems your admiration has blinded you to the truth.

☛ *Go to Section 54.*

32

You propose the Tangeys' poverty as a clear motive and their occupation at the Foreign Office as their means of accessing the treaty. Mrs Tangey's behaviour on the night of the theft was particularly suspicious.

Forbes's disappointment is evident. He shares your suspicions regarding Mrs Tangey and had hoped you would produce some incontrovertible evidence.

'With the greatest of respect, Mr Holmes, we've already made the Tangeys' life a misery. We took their home apart and questioned them both for hours. If they're hiding anything from us, well, I'd say they are better diplomatists than the Foreign Secretary himself.'

As you make your way back to Baker Street, Watson offers to return to Briarbrae on the morrow to inform Percy of your failure.

THE END

33

Lord Holdhurst

In Downing Street, you navigate a sea of obstructive civil servants until you find yourself face-to-face with the Foreign Minister. Lord Holdhurst might be unimpressed by your disregard for protocol but he greets you civilly.

He is a tall, stately man and clearly very intelligent, but one small detail cannot escape your attention: the soles of his boots have been re-soled, indicating that he is not as wealthy as his position might suggest.

'Your name is very familiar to me, Mr Holmes,' he says, 'and, of course, I cannot pretend to be ignorant of the object of your visit. There has only been one occurrence in these offices which could call for your attention. In whose interest are you acting, may I ask?'

'In that of Mr Percy Phelps,' you reply. 'I wonder if you might outline the events surrounding the occurrence.'

'On the evening of 23 May, I commissioned my nephew to make a copy of a very secret document: a naval treaty between Great Britain and the Kingdom of Italy. I instructed that he should wait until he was alone before commencing the work and return the documents to my safe upon completion.

'That same night I was awoken by a commotion at my door and representatives from Scotland Yard who informed me that the treaty had been stolen.'

'Percy had been robbed?' gasps Watson.

'Not at all,' replies Holdhurst. 'According to his account, he had asked the commissionaire's wife for a cup of coffee. When it failed to arrive, he went down to the commissionaire's office, found the man asleep and the bell to his own room ringing. When he returned to his desk, the document was missing.'

It is clear that Lord Holdhurst is less than impressed by his nephew's account.

☛ *Would you like to see the room where the theft occurred? If so, go to Section 56.*

☛ *Or perhaps you would prefer to question Lord Holdhurst further, in which case go to Section 17.*

34

You ask Forbes about the commissionaire and his wife.

'Mr Tangey has been shadowed. He left the Guards with a good character and we can find nothing against him. His wife is a bad lot, though. I fancy she knows more about this than appears. She drinks and we have interrogated her twice when she was in her cups but we could get nothing out of her, other than that she had brokers in the house. But they were paid off.'

'Where did the money come from?'

'Mr Tangey's pension. We checked the funds were all in order.'

'What explanation did she give of having answered the bell when Mr Phelps rang for the coffee?'

'She said that her husband was very tired and she wished to relieve him.'

'Did you ask why she hurried away that night?'

'She was later than usual and wanted to get home.'

'And she was at home when you and Mr Phelps called on her that night?'

'No, we arrived at the Tangey household just before she arrived.'

'How much of a head start did she have?'

'About twenty minutes but she explained that by the difference between a 'bus and a hansom.'

'How did she react when she discovered you waiting for her?'

'She ran into the back kitchen - apparently because she had the money there with which to pay off the brokers.'

'Did you ask her whether she met anyone or saw anyone loitering about Charles Street?'

'She saw no one but the constable on duty.'

Mrs Tangey seems to have an answer for everything.

☛ If you would like to ask Forbes about Charles Gorot, go to Section 19.

☛ If you want to return to Woking immediately, go to Section 39.

Percy's future brother-in-law is a vulgar man with a veneer of forced joviality. He has made a comfortable life for himself here at Briarbrae but is unlikely to be welcome in perpetuity.

Did he have the means and a motive to steal the naval treaty?

Clearly something has aroused your suspicions.

☛ *Was it a bell? If so, go to Section 4.*

☛ *Or a monogram? If so, go to Section 44.*

36

Even if Miss Harrison had a motive to hurt her fiancé, she was not in London on the night of the theft. One of Briarbrae's residents must have hidden the treaty in the room but, now it has been found, you have no way to winkle out the guilty party.

Percy and Annie are overjoyed that the treaty has been recovered and you allow yourself to bask in their gratitude a moment before departing for London.

The Foreign Office is equally grateful. No one wants to pursue a criminal investigation because they would prefer to keep the incident out of the public eye.

You find it hard to find satisfaction in this half-baked resolution, but at least your reputation has not been diminished.

THE END

37

'I should warn you, Mr Holmes, the lady of the house is unlikely to be friendly,' says Forbes. 'She is overly fond of drink and was having money problems even before her husband's employment was thrown into jeopardy.'

Forbes has brought you to a rundown tenement in a rundown corner of town. You knock on the dilapidated door and it is answered by a dilapidated, red-faced woman.

You introduce yourself, reassuring Mrs Tangey that she is not being investigated a second time. Mr Tangey, slouching in his threadbare chair beside a cold fire, looks thoroughly miserable.

You ask him to recount the events of the night that the document went missing.

'I was watching the main entrance when Mr Phelps rang the bell. My wife was about to head home but, instead, she went upstairs to see Mr Phelps and then told me that he wanted a cup of strong coffee. I'm ashamed to say that I was derelict. He later came down to my office and found me asleep. As I awoke, the bell from Mr Phelps's office rang again, even though he was standing right beside me at that moment. We hastened upstairs but there was no one there and his document had gone!'

Mrs Tangey adds, 'And o' course, Mr Phelps thinks it was us that took the blessed thing. They turned this place upside down!'

You nod sympathetically. 'At what time did you leave the building that night, Mrs Tangey?'

'Shortly after I asked Mr Tangey to make the coffee. I was in a hurry; it had just started to rain.'

'And you left through the front entrance?'

'No, through the side entrance into the lane.'

The dispirited Mr Tangey mumbles to himself, 'It makes no sense. Why would the thief announce themself by ringing the bell?'

Mrs Tangey

☞ *Why indeed? You decide it is time to visit your client in Woking. Go to Section 40.*

38

As you search the room, you ask Percy Phelps, 'How long have you used this room as a bedchamber?'

'For the past nine weeks.'

'And before then?'

'I slept upstairs. I exchanged rooms with Joseph when my brain-fever took hold.'

You examine the window and note that the intruder must have used a blade to prise it open.

'Do you think you could walk round the house with me?' you ask.

'Oh, yes,' he enthuses. 'I should like a little sunshine. Joseph will come too.'

Annie Harrison wishes to accompany you but you instinctively ask her to remain in the room. She accepts this with bad grace.

Outside you note marks on the flower bed beneath Percy's window but they are too faint to tell you anything.

You ponder why Percy's room was chosen by the burglar, given that the windows to the drawing room and dining room are both larger and would have offered richer pickings.

'Perhaps because those windows are more visible from the road,' Mr Harrison suggests.

Joseph takes you to the place on the perimeter where he believes the intruder scaled the fence. One of the wooden rails has certainly been cracked and you examine a fragment of wood. It has been damaged recently from the interior. You continue towards the main gate.

'Do you have any plate in the house that might entice a burglar?' you ask.

'Nothing of value,' replies Percy.

On the other side of the fence, where the rail had been cracked, you can find no evidence of it being scaled. Perhaps the intruder did not have to climb the fence at all.

> ☛ *It is time to get to the bottom of*
> *this affair. Go to Section 21.*

39

When you return to Briarbrae, Percy Phelps appears to be in better health but both he and Miss Harrison are clearly agitated.

'Mr Holmes, we have had an adventure during the night, and one which might have proved to be a serious one. I believe I may be the unconscious centre of some monstrous conspiracy and that my life is aimed at, as well as my honour. It sounds incredible, for I have not, as far as I know, an enemy in the world. Yet, from last night's experience I can come to no other conclusion.'

'Someone tried to break into Percy's room,' clarifies Miss Harrison.

Percy Phelps resumes his narrative:

'Last night was the very first night that I have ever slept without a nurse in the room. I was so much better that I thought I could dispense with one. I had a night-light burning, however. Well, about two in the morning, I had sunk into a light sleep when I was suddenly aroused by a slight noise. It was like the sound a mouse makes when it is gnawing a plank and I lay listening to it for some time under the impression that it must come from that cause.

Then it grew louder and, suddenly, there came from the window a sharp metallic snick. I sat up in amazement. There could be no doubt what the sounds were now. The first ones had been caused by someone forcing an instrument through the slit between the sashes and the second by the catch being pressed back.

'There was a pause then for about ten minutes, as if the person were waiting to see whether the noise had awakened me. Then I heard a gentle creaking as the window was very slowly opened. I could stand it no longer, for my nerves are not what they used to be. I sprang out of bed and flung open the shutters. A man was crouching at the window and ran off into the night.'

This is a curious development.

> ☞ *If you want to search for physical evidence, go to Section 38.*
>
> ☞ *If you would rather allow Percy Phelps to continue his narrative, go to Section 3.*

40

The train from Waterloo pulls into Woking just after noon. Briarbrae is only a few minutes' walk away and you soon find yourself at the door of a large, detached house overlooking an impressive estate. The housekeeper takes your cards and bids you wait in the hall.

A few minutes later you are joined by a young woman with thick black hair and dark eyes. Could this be the scribe of Percy Phelps'szz letter?

'Oh, Mr Holmes, thank goodness!' she exclaims. 'I am Annie Harrison, Percy's fiancée. Please come with me.'

Miss Harrison shows you to a room on the ground floor that has been converted into a bedchamber. A very pale man lies on the sofa, his face lined with anxiety.

This is undoubtedly your client. A plump, ruddy-faced gentleman stands beside him and favours you with an impish smile as you enter the room. He introduces himself as Joseph, Annie's brother.

Watson greets his old schoolmate and introduces you.

'Mr Holmes, I do not know where to begin ...' Percy Phelps moans.

Annie Harrison

'Be at ease, Mr Phelps,' you reply. 'I am apprised of the events surrounding the loss of the naval treaty and shall endeavour to assist in its recovery.'

You take some satisfaction from Percy's speechless astonishment. It is Annie who breaks the protracted silence.

'Your reputation is well-deserved, Mr Holmes, but there has been a development that might complicate your investigation. Last night someone attempted to break into Percy's room.'

'Was anything taken?' you ask.

'No, the intruder evidently thought Percy asleep and, when he cried out, they escaped back through the window.'

This is an interesting complication. How will you untangle it?

☞ *If you want to examine the sickroom, head to Section 38.*

☞ *If you would prefer to question Percy Phelps, go to Section 3.*

41

One person who was irrefutably present at the time of the theft was Percy Phelps. He has been a virtual recluse for the past two months, but is his 'brain-fever' an elaborate cover?

You summon the constabulary to Briarbrae before making your pronouncement.

What has raised your suspicions?

☞ *The letter? Go to Section 43.*

☞ *The sickroom? Go to Section 48.*

42

You return to Baker Street, bloodied but triumphant. Despite your client's fragile state of mind, you cannot resist a final dramatic touch.

Meeting Mrs Hudson as she prepares to bring in the tea and coffee, you slip the treaty into an empty covered dish. Your indefatigable landlady knows better than to ask what you are up to.

When you enter the room, Phelps resembles a forlorn puppy and it requires considerable discipline to prevent a grin from spoiling what you hope is a concerned frown.

Watson regards your bandaged hand but you wave away his concern. Both men are clearly eager for news of your adventures.

Instead, you encourage your guest to help himself to the delicious breakfast of curried chicken that Mrs Hudson has prepared. To your immense disappointment he declares he has no appetite and so, raising your injured hand significantly, you ask if he wouldn't mind assisting you.

Percy Phelps raises the cover of the indicated dish and lets out a scream.

The sight of the naval treaty almost causes him to faint and Watson jumps up to steady his old school fellow, who stares at you with a mixture of amazement and gratitude.

'God bless you, Mr Holmes. You have saved my honour!'

You sit down to a well-earned breakfast and start to recount last night's events with a sense of considerable satisfaction.

THE END

Phelps must
have anticipated
your powers of
handwriting
analysis, which is
why he dictated
his plea to his
fiancée. Doubtless
he involved you to
divert suspicion.

The London Chronicle

FROM THURSDAY AUGUST 8, TO SATURDAY AUGUST 12, 1981

WAR

You formally
accuse Phelps of
taking the treaty. He
responds by fainting
on the spot and has to be taken into custody on a stretcher.

After as thorough an interrogation as they are able to inflict
on the gibbering prisoner, the police are no closer to ascertaining
the whereabouts of the treaty but they use emergency measures
to detain Phelps, whose health goes into even steeper decline as
a result.

A week later you hear from your brother Mycroft that the treaty
had fallen into the hands of the Russians. As a result Britain is now
on the brink of war. Percy Phelps is released and transferred to an
asylum.

Your brother sums up the case thus: 'You have ruined the life of
an innocent man and failed to prevent an international catastrophe.
Perhaps you should refrain from meddling in affairs of State and
stick to your chemistry set in future.'

THE END

44

Joseph's pendant bearing the monogram 'J.H.' speaks of a man with a taste for the finer things in life but his situation at Briarbrae, despite its connections to the aristocracy, is far from optimal.

Selling the treaty to one of Britain's rivals would certainly make him wealthier but if the transaction had already been made, its repercussions would have reached the Foreign Office by now.

If he did take the treaty, where is it now?

☛ *If you think it is at the Foreign Office, go to Section 13.*

☛ *If you believe it is in Briarbrae, go to Section 16.*

45

Convinced that the treaty is in Percy's room, you need to remove him from Briarbrae so the thief might again be tempted to retrieve their plunder.

You suggest that Percy spends the night in the spare room at Baker Street and he is greatly relieved by your proposal.

'Would you prefer that Joseph comes with us to look after me?' he asks.

You decline the offer, assuring Phelps that Watson will be able to attend to his needs. Before you leave Briarbrae you have a private word with Annie Harrison. You request that she remains in Percy's sickroom for the rest of the day and locks it behind her when she retires. As you hoped, she agrees without question.

At Woking Station Phelps and Watson are surprised when you reveal that you will not be accompanying them. With the two men on their way to London, you proceed to the nearby village of Ripley, where you are able to procure a flask of coffee and some sandwiches.

When evening falls, you make your way back to Briarbrae. Just after sunset you scale the fence and make your way across the grounds under the cover of darkness to a clump of rhododendrons not far from the window of Phelps's sickroom. The blinds are not down so you are able to observe Annie Harrison reading at the table.

The night is not cold but the hours crawl by. Finally, at a quarter past ten, Miss Harrison puts down her book, closes the blinds and leaves the room. You hear her closing the door and turning the key in the lock.

The church clock keeps you informed of each drawn-out 15-minute interval. It is the only salient sound other than the occasional bark of a fox or the hoot of an owl.

It is almost two in the
morning before your vigil is
rewarded and a shadowy figure
approaches the window, which he
proceeds to jemmy with a blade.
You watch as he climbs through the
opening and walks purposely to the door,
where he kneels down, peels back the carpet
and removes one of the floorboards. Having
recovered his objective the intruder leaves by the
same route.

In the darkness you confront the surprised burglar,
who lashes out with his blade. Your reflexes have been
somewhat dampened from the hours squatting under a bush
and you sustain a stinging cut to your arm before you are able to
bring your superior martial prowess to bear.

Breathless and beaten, Joseph Harrison glares at you, then
begins a plea, which you cut short by holding out your hand.

He gives you the cylinder of paper and, in the second that it
takes you to confirm that it is, indeed, the naval treaty, he springs
up and runs into the night. You decide that the recovery of the
document outweighs the need to risk further misadventure by
pursuing the thief. Mr
Forbes and his colleagues
can have the pleasure
of pursuing the luckless
fugitive.

*How would you like to
conclude the case?*

☛ *With a dramatic flourish?*
Go to Section 42.

☛ *Or with appropriate decorum?*
Go to Section 50.

46

You take a cab to Downing Street to meet the Foreign Minister in his chambers.

Lord Holdhurst greets you with old-fashioned courtesy and invites Watson and yourself to take a seat on either side of the fireplace. He stands between you, radiating the authority of his office.

Tall and slender, with a head of curly, prematurely greying hair and a shrewd face, the Foreign Minister is every inch the nobleman, but you notice that his boots have been re-soled. Lord Holdhurst's wealth is not commensurate with his station.

He knows you by reputation and has already deduced the reason for your visit. 'You have come at the behest of my nephew regarding the missing naval treaty. Please ask your questions, Mr Holmes.'

'Did you tell anyone that you intended to commission a copy of the treaty?'

'No one.'

So it is possible that the thief's presence was accidental. He saw his chance and he took it, you think.

Lord Holdhurst

'Am I right in thinking that grave results would follow if the details of this treaty became known?' you ask.

'Very grave results, indeed.'

'And have they occurred?'

'Not yet.'

'If the treaty had reached the French or Russian Foreign Office, you would expect to hear of it?'

'I should,' replies Lord Holdhurst wryly.

'Since nearly ten weeks have elapsed and nothing has been heard, it's fair to suppose that the treaty has not yet reached them.'

Lord Holdhurst shrugs. 'But we can hardly suppose, Mr Holmes, that the thief took the treaty in order to frame it and hang it up.'

'Perhaps he is waiting for a better price,' you suggest.

'If he waits a little longer, he will get no price at all. The treaty will cease to be secret in a few months.'

'Of course, it is a possible supposition that the thief has had a sudden illness ...'

'An attack of brain-fever, for example?' interjects Holdhurst.

'I did not say so,' you reply. 'And now, Lord Holdhurst, we have already taken up too much of your valuable time so we shall wish you good day.'

☞ *You now have sufficient information. It is time to return to Woking. Go to Section 39.*

47

Charles Gorot was one of the last people to communicate with Phelps before the treaty was stolen and his surname links him to France, one of the countries that would benefit most from obtaining the treaty.

Mr Forbes is less than impressed.

'We have already questioned Mr Gorot,' says the detective. 'He can account for his movements after leaving the office and we did a thorough search of his dwelling. If that's the best you've got, Mr Holmes, I'm afraid our correspondence has reached its conclusion. If you will excuse me, gentlemen, I have some detective work to attend to.'

Watson puts away his notebook, a signal that this case will not be recorded as one of your successes.

THE END

48

Phelps has not left his sickroom for the past two months. Could he have had the treaty in his possession all this time? You convey your suspicions to the police, and a protesting Percy is removed from the room so that officers can conduct a thorough search.

They initially turn up nothing but you notice an irregularity in the floorboards. Prising one of the planks reveals a makeshift hidden compartment containing a scroll of paper.

You present the treaty to Percy and his indignance melts into a look of sheer horror. 'It was in my room all this time? How ...'

As the constables move to apprehend Percy Phelps, he appears closer to a complete mental breakdown than ever. He turns to you with wide, desperate eyes. 'Please, Mr Holmes, I didn't take it, I swear!'

Are you sure you have the right man?

☛ *Yes? There is sufficient evidence to convict him. Proceed to Section 24.*

☛ *No? You've made a foolish mistake. Retreat to Section 30.*

49

'Mr Harrison is using one of the upstairs rooms, is that correct?'

'Yes. He's using mine. We exchanged rooms after I became ill.'

'So prior to that, he had been sleeping here.'

'Mr Holmes, I don't see where you are ...'

'Where is Mr Harrison now?' you enquire.

'He said he had urgent business in town and left just before you arrived.'

You politely ask Percy to leave his bed while you conduct a thorough search of his room. The thief proves to be a master of concealment but, ultimately, no match for you. The treaty is cunningly hidden in a secret compartment beneath a loose floorboard.

When you present it to Percy Phelps, he and his fiancée are overcome with relief and gratitude. With some embarrassment you extract yourself from their overpowering appreciation (and promises of a wedding invitation) and take the treaty back to the Foreign Office.

Lord Holdhurst is equally appreciative but, thankfully, more restrained in his expression.

'Have you apprehended the thief?' he asks.

'I regret not.'

'That may be a blessing,' he says with a wry smile. 'It would be better for all concerned if this affair were kept out of the courts - and the papers.' Before you turn to leave, he adds, 'Our nation owes you a debt of gratitude, Mr Holmes. A very good day to you.'

THE END

50

You take the first available train back to Waterloo and, from there, directly to the Foreign Office.

Lord Holdhurst does not keep you waiting and is visibly delighted when you produce the treaty.

'You have almost certainly saved us from a costly war, Mr Holmes,' he says.

Or postponed the inevitable, you think, wisely keeping the opinion to yourself.

That evening you go out to dine with your brother Mycroft. His reluctance to give you credit is as strong as ever but the marked absence of critique or sarcasm is as close as he has ever come to fraternal affection.

'Have you ever considered a career in politics, Sherlock?' he asks.

THE END

51

Clearly the thief knew that there was something of value in Percy's room. Annie is certainly a strong-willed woman with the vigour of youth, but do you really see her as a knife-wielding burglar?

☛ *Yes? She only married Phelps to improve her status. Go to Section 54.*

☛ *No? You stand by your original assessment of her good character. Go to Section 36.*

52

'Which train did you intend to take back to Woking?' you ask.

'The 11 o'clock. I had planned to travel back with Joseph,' said Phelps.

'Did you tell anyone you had a special task to perform?'

'No one.'

'Not Miss Harrison here, for example?'

'No. I had not been back to Woking between getting the order and executing the commission.'

'What transpired when you returned to Woking?'

'The prospect of losing everything consumed my wits and I contracted brain-fever. I have been as you see me these past nine weeks. Lord Holdhurst wrote to me to reiterate that the recovery of the treaty was of the utmost importance and added that no steps would be taken about my future - by which he means, of course, my dismissal - until my health was restored and I had an opportunity of repairing my misfortune.'

You pause to consider suspects, motivations and means.

Your contemplations are broken by Miss Harrison.

'Do you see any prospect of solving this mystery, Mr Holmes? Do you suspect someone?'

'I suspect myself ... of coming to conclusions too rapidly.'

She is clearly unimpressed. 'Then go to London,' she says, 'and test your conclusions.'

☛ *Miss Harrison's advice is excellent. It is time to return to London. Go to Section 14.*

53

No one was closer to Percy Phelps than his future wife. She has been his nursemaid in this room for the past nine weeks. And what better place to hide the treaty than right here?

You order a complete search of the room. After an hour you find nothing but, just as Phelps finds the courage to protest, you notice a curious irregularity in the floorboards. Prising one of the planks reveals a makeshift hidden compartment containing a scroll of paper.

The treaty had been beneath their feet all along!

What confirmed your suspicions?

☞ *The letter? Go to Section 31.*

☞ *The break-in? Go to Section 51.*

54

As Annie is led away by the constables, Percy Phelps is inconsolable. His relief at the recovery of the treaty is utterly eclipsed by the heartbreak of her betrayal.

On your journey back to London, you are haunted by a nagging doubt, which becomes fully corporeal a week later when you receive an unsigned letter:

> It is a terrible injustice that my sister should be punished for my misdeeds. Though I deeply regret hurting her, I will not throw myself on the mercy of the law.
>
> I do not seek forgiveness but please use your powers to convince the authorities of her innocence and persuade Percy to take her back. Though she shares my blood, our hearts could not be more unalike.

You review the evidence and realise that you made a grave oversight. Perhaps you can help to put things right, although you doubt that the denizens of Briarbrae will want anything to do with you now.

A diplomatic disaster has been averted, but your blunder has caused unnecessary pain to an innocent man and woman.

THE END

55

Your brother possesses an analytical talent that surpasses your own but he lacks the tenacious energy required for detective work, which is just as well as you have grown used to your unrivalled status in the field. He is, however, well-placed in the government.

A cab takes you to Whitehall and you meet Mycroft at his clubhouse. He shakes your hand with a pudgy paw and subjects you to his customary forensic scrutiny.

'Hello, Sherlock. Evidently, you have not come here for a familial tête-à-tête. There are innumerable affairs of State that would benefit from your specialised attention, but I will hazard a guess that your objective is the naval treaty that has gone missing from the Foreign Office. Am I far off the mark?'

'Not by so much as a degree,' you concede.

'Your client is Lord Holdhurst?' Mycroft looks almost impressed.

'Not directly. One of his underlings by the name of Phelps.'

'Ah, the poor wretch who mislaid the document. Have you any suspects?'

'I have yet to cast my net but I wondered if you might give me your impression of the Foreign Secretary.'

Mycroft scowls. 'Tread carefully, Sherlock. Lord Holdhurst could well be our next Prime Minister. If you are asking me to reveal some impropriety, I must disappoint you. I can offer you some intelligence, however: the Foreign Minister is most certainly not your thief.'

You trust your brother's judgement, although his motivations are often inscrutable.

It seems likely that Phelps's consternation is directly connected to this missing naval treaty.

Where will you look for answers?

☛ *If you would prefer to ignore Mycroft's advice and confront Lord Holdhurst, go to Section 33.*

☛ *If you decide to go to Woking and meet your client, go to Section 25.*

56

Lord Holdhurst takes you to a large, open room of about sixty square feet.

You ask him to show you the precise location where he gave Phelps the commission.

'Right here,' replies the Foreign Secretary, standing almost exactly in the centre of the room.

'Then you could hardly have been overheard?'

'It is out of the question; what's more, we were the only ones present and speaking in little more than a whisper.'

'Would you be so kind as to show me to Mr Phelps's room?' you ask.

Lord Holdhurst accompanies you to another building. You enter through the main door and walk down a long hall, noting the commissionaire's office to your right. At the end of the hall is a flight of stairs leading straight up to a landing with two doors. One is a side entrance, which leads downstairs to the lane outside; the

Charles Gorot

other leads to another stairwell, which takes you up to the clerks' room.

A single clerk is working at his desk. Lord Holdhurst introduces him as Charles Gorot.

'Mr Gorot was working here on the night of the theft. He went home before my nephew commenced work on the copy and has satisfied the police regarding his whereabouts.'

'And the commissionaire, I take it he has been questioned?'

'Yes. His name is Tangey. He and his wife were interrogated at length by Mr Forbes of Scotland Yard. They were the most obvious suspects, but the police could find nothing to incriminate them.'

☞ *If you would like to visit Mr Forbes, go to Section 11.*

☞ *If you decide it is time to visit the client in Woking, go to Section 40.*

THE FINAL PROBLEM

1

Friday, 24 April 1891.

'Oh, what's the use!' says a clearly exasperated Mrs Hudson. She has been talking for almost seven minutes but your mind was engaged elsewhere. One word, however, broke into your thoughts.

'Use?' you murmur. But she has already collected the tray of untouched tea and closed the door behind her.

As you look down from your drawing-room window onto the mid-morning bustle of Baker Street, you consider the word in relation to yourself.

To your esteemed friend and colleague Dr John Watson, your use as a companion and a source of stimulation has greatly diminished of late. He has cheerfully succumbed to married life and his medical practice is flourishing. He has little use for Sherlock Holmes.

To the city of London, you have been so useful in ridding it of its human vermin as to make yourself ultimately redundant. All of your foes have been vanquished, bar one. And soon this last villain will be brought to justice and your great work completed.

What was that?

The tiniest creak of a board on the stairs. It is not Mrs Hudson, who you can hear stoically going about her business in the scullery. Someone has entered your home without alerting your landlady.

You open a draw and remove a small pistol, which you conceal in the pocket of your dressing gown as the door handle starts to turn.

☛ *Prepare to meet the intruder in Section 3.*

2

You decide to go on foot - a brisk half-hour walk will help to marshal your thoughts. But as you get closer to Watson's neighbourhood, you have the overwhelming sensation of being followed. The feeling intensifies as you cross Piccadilly until you turn a corner and come face to face with a tall, heavy-set man. His scarred features indicate that he is no stranger to violence and the malevolent grin suggests he is eager to renew the acquaintance.

   The footsteps of your pursuer increase their pace behind you, while the brute before you produces a vicious-looking cudgel, pitted and spattered from frequent use.

There is no chance of talking your way out of this. What do you do?

☛ *Fight? Go to Section 13.*

☛ *Flee? Go to Section 27.*

3

The door is flung open and the figure of a man stands before you. He is tall and thin, clean-shaven and pale, with a great domed forehead and shoulders rounded from much study. His face protrudes and moves slowly, like a reptile. Deep-set eyes subject you to a swift but meticulous analysis before he speaks:

'You have less frontal development than I should have expected. It is a dangerous habit to finger loaded firearms in the pocket of one's dressing gown.'

Impressed by his perspicacity, you remove the weapon and place it, still cocked, on the table.

'Evidently, you do not know me,' he says.

He is wrong. The face may be unfamiliar but you had been thinking of this man mere minutes ago. Standing before you, in your own home, is the spider at the dark heart of London's iniquitous web, the Napoleon of crime: Professor Moriarty.

'On the contrary,' you reply. 'Please take a chair. I can spare you five minutes if you have anything to say.'

'All that I have to say has already crossed your mind.'

'Then, possibly, my answer has crossed yours.'

'You must drop it, Mr Holmes. You really must, you know. It has been an intellectual treat to watch you grapple with my affairs and it would be a grief to me to be forced to take extreme measures.'

'Danger is part of my trade,' you reply.

'I do not speak of danger but your utter destruction. You hope to put me in the dock but I assure you that will never happen. You have secured your own demise by crossing me.'

His eyes seem to burn, evaluating you as an owl might assess a mouse trapped beneath its claws. You feel as if your very soul has been violated by the inspection. Then, without another word, he leaves.

Moriarty

☞ *This changes everything.*
Go to Section 11.

4

The *Illuminati* have a number of safehouses across the continent. With a vicious criminal mastermind on your tail, you do not think it too presumptuous to avail yourself of the order's hospitality. When you finally arrive in Paris, your lodgings is a spartan bunk-bed dormitory within a former masonic lodge.

During this respite you send a telegraph to Scotland Yard and receive a reply the same day informing you that Moriarty's London gang have been apprehended but that the professor is still at large. This comes as no surprise - he is most certainly here.

You try to persuade Watson to return to England but he refuses to abandon you.

When you feel suitably restored, you decide to move on. Your status with the *Illuminati* is tenuous and you are sure that if Professor Moriarty is reluctant to attack you on this hallowed ground, he will have no such compunctions in the backstreets of Paris.

☞ *Take the next train to Switzerland in Section 47.*

5

You rush towards the figure, hoping that your momentum will have an intimidating effect to counteract the distance you need to cover.

Unfortunately, it creates no such reaction. The figure stands their ground and produces an object that, although obscured by shadows, can only be a revolver.

You are almost within striking distance when you hear the click of the trigger. There is no time to berate yourself for running towards certain death. A blinding flash is accompanied by a deafening bang that reverberates down the narrow passage.

☞ *Meet your fate in Section 26.*

6

The daylight is starting to fade as you approach Watson's home. You knock on the door with some force, all the time looking about you to ensure you have not brought devils to your friend's threshold.

The doctor opens the door and his eyes open wide with surprise.

'Holmes! Good heavens, man, you look terrible!'

'Yes, I have been using myself up rather too freely,' you respond as calmly as you can. He ushers you in with a concern that is both professional and sympathetic.

Moving to the window you ask, 'Have you any objection to my closing your shutters?'

Watson nods his consent. Edging round the wall you bring the shutters together and bolt them securely.

'Whatever is the matter? Are you afraid of something?' he asks.

'Indeed, I am, Watson. Are you alone?'

'Yes, Mary is away visiting.'

'And your practice?'

'Quiet at the moment.'

'Then I would like to propose that you come with me for a week to the continent.'

'Where?'

'Oh, anywhere. It's all the same to me.'

The bafflement that creases your friend's features is more than you can bear so you explain the situation

from the very beginning. That most of London's organised crime has been orchestrated by one Professor Moriarty is news to Watson but the fact that you are now directly pitted against the professor turns his perplexity to anxiety.

'The police will engage Moriarty's gang here in town,' you conclude, 'but he will make me his primary target. So I propose we take the express to Paris and decide our ongoing itinerary on the way.'

'You will spend the night here?' asks Watson.

'No, my friend. I fear I would be a dangerous guest.' You open the back door and enter the garden. 'I shall see you tomorrow at the station. Goodnight, Watson.'

Before he can raise an objection, you clamber over the garden wall and land, less cat-like than you hoped, in Mortimer Street.

☞ *There is time to find a disguise and lodgings for the night before going to the station in Section 28.*

7

From Dieppe you continue to Brussels and take a room there for the night before moving on to Strasbourg. In the morning you send a telegraph to Scotland Yard and, after a day of somewhat strained sightseeing, you return to your hotel to find their reply, which you share with Watson.

'Moriarty's London gang have been rounded up but their leader has slipped the net. It may have been naïve to expect the Parisian police to go the extra mile in order to apprehend a foreign national. I think that you had better return to England, Watson.'

'Why?'

'Because you will find me a dangerous companion now. We have broken Moriarty's circle and he will be set on avenging himself.'

'You cannot seriously believe that I would abandon you at this juncture.'

You look into the doctor's eyes and see a resolve that will brook no argument.

'Very well. The professor will have realised our deception by now and calculated our actual destination. I propose that we remain in motion.'

☛ *If you continue to Switzerland, go to Section 47.*

☛ 👁 *If you feel like a trip to Bavaria, go to Section 21.*

8

At no point during your career as a consulting detective did you include 'martyr' in your list of ambitions. In a heartbeat you gladly sacrifice both courage and reason on the altar of self-preservation and make a run for it!

Moriarty's enraged visage is imprinted on your mind as you hurry back along the Alpine path. But which way to go?

If you return to Meiringen, you risk bringing calamity on Herr Steiler and his guests. Perhaps you could find your way to Rosenlaui and lie low there?

As you consider your very limited options, reason returns and draws your attention to the fact that you are standing out in the open, surrounded by various rocky elevations that would perfectly serve as a concealed position for a marksman.

The realisation comes too late. You do not hear the shot but, curiously, have time to ponder that the professor's assassin most likely used a high-powered air rifle.

The bullet is, quite literally, the last thing to go through your brilliant mind.

THE END

9

Paris shares many similarities with London - crowded districts, social inequality and an active criminal underworld. Despite this pleasant familiarity you feel decidedly unsafe.

You attempt to mitigate the feeling by putting up in the best hotel you can find. It is clear that Watson shares your unease when you sit down to supper, which has been brought up to your room.

The doctor has been more conscious of his dietary regimen since getting married and declines some of the richer morsels, including the wine. You normally sustain yourself on very little but your appetite is oddly enhanced today.

It must have been the wine that was laced with poison. You might have detected it if your palate had not been overloaded by the cuisine. You topple backwards and do not even feel the impact when your head hits the floor.

Watson's visage is grotesquely cracked. The poor fellow looks as if he is about to burst into tears. You watch with detached amusement as he desperately unbuttons your shirt and exhausts his repertoire of skills in an attempt to save your life. It would be churlish to tell a professional physician that he is wasting his time so you refrain from doing so. The sensation you are experiencing is not entirely alien; it recalls the fevered dreams brought on by the milk of the poppy. Everything starts to fade and you regret that you forgot to say goodbye because this is ...

THE END

10

There is no doubt that Professor Moriarty will put his plans against you into immediate effect. Lying low at home is not an option so you set off for Watson's house on foot.

A few streets from your destination, you sense that someone is following you. Quickening your pace, you glance back, then sidestep into a narrow alley.

Your pursuer is around 6ft and 200lb and his heavy footsteps continue to approach at a constant pace. There is no certainty that this man wishes you harm so you dismiss the notion of ambushing him and instead go deeper into the filthy, tunnel-like alley. Just as you reach the middle, a figure appears at the other end. The newcomer is slightly built but their stance suggests they are not to be trifled with.

Turning around you see your heavier pursuer has also entered the alley. If there were any doubts as to his intentions, the huge cudgel in his right hand puts them to rest. You are trapped.

What will you do?

☛ *Take your chances with the brute?*
Go to Section 37.

☛ *Or charge towards the other figure? Go to Section 5.*

11

Professor Moriarty's threat cannot be taken lightly but you will not lock yourself inside 221b like a craven!

Your adversary is a meticulous strategist and his schemes have evaded your investigative powers for many years. However, given enough time even an intellectual titan will make a mistake and that is precisely what happened this year: Moriarty crossed swords with an adversary every bit as guileful as himself and they have chosen you to be the engine of his destruction.

For the last three months you have worked to undermine his schemes. Very soon you will have sufficient evidence to bring down his entire hive and it is essential that it be delivered to the authorities with all haste. Unfortunately, Scotland Yard would demand to know the source of your evidence, which would not suit your informant, so you must climb to a higher rung, where no questions will be asked - the shadowy sub-section of Her Majesty's government that is the domain of your brother Mycroft.

He will be at his Pall Mall residence this afternoon, so you decide to make the journey on foot. Walking down Baker Street you allow no outward signs of apprehension to show but your senses are excruciatingly heightened - every passer-by could be an enemy.

By the time you reach Welbeck Street, you are in a more relaxed frame of mind, and you are just crossing the road when a two-horse van appears from seemingly nowhere and accelerates towards you on a collision course. Only your well-honed reflexes save you and you leap onto the footpath at the very last moment. The van disappears around a corner, leaving you alone and shaken in the empty street.

You are still trying to recover your equilibrium as you hasten down Vere Street. It proves to be a sensible change of pace - a large brick topples from one of the rooftops and smashes into the pavement beside you, narrowly avoiding crushing your skull to a pulp.

Only a fool would attribute two near-death experiences to coincidence. You decide to abandon this perilous perambulation.

☛ *Will you hail a cab and continue to your brother's residence? If so, go to Section 15.*

☛ *Dr Watson's House is considerably closer. If you would rather go there, go to Section 10.*

12

The *Illuminati* was founded in Bavaria almost exactly 115 years ago. Its declared goal was to rid the world of superstition and corruption. You use the handbook, given to you when you were inducted into the order to locate their Munich headquarters. The building is nondescript and located away from the populous centre of town.

Using a succession of passwords and cryptograms, you are eventually given an audience with a man who introduces himself as 'Brother Spartacus'.

'We wondered when you would see fit to visit us,' he says with a bland half-smile.

'I wish to discuss your decision to crown Professor Moriarty the "king of organised crime" in London.'

The metaphor clearly rankles Spartacus as you had hoped. Before he can object, you press on: 'You believe you can control Moriarty and perhaps mitigate the effects of crime on society, but I suggest that your interference will have the opposite effect. The distinction between medieval monarchs and modern extortionists is infinitesimally narrow. If you allow Moriarty to flourish, his criminal empire will not only stifle social reform but pull London inexorably back into the Dark Ages.'

'On what do you base your prognosis?'

'On a lifetime of work dedicated to studying the minds and behaviour of men like Moriarty.'

Brother Spartacus

'Is that all you wish to say?'

'Moriarty's gang have been apprehended by Scotland Yard. Only his inner circle remains. I once shared your admiration for the professor's singular abilities but I have stripped him of his limbs and soon I shall have his head.'

Looking the leader of the century-old secret society in the eye, you see him evaluate his remaining options and realise he has none.

'You have bested us, Mr Holmes, and we shall always be glad to call you a fellow Illuminatus. Allow us to take care of the professor so you may return to London in peace.'

THE END

13

Your would-be assassin raises the club above his head and bellows. Doubtless this has terrified many of his victims prior to their bloody demise but you are not so easily daunted. You deliver a swift right jab to his face that sends a jolt of pain down your forearm but rewards you with the satisfying sensation of his rotten teeth giving way to your fist. His roar becomes a gurgled yelp and the brute staggers backwards.

The sound of his accomplice rapidly approaching convinces you it is time to leave. You race through the streets, glad of your intimate acquaintance with the area's back alleys and shortcuts, and you are greatly relieved when Watson's house finally comes into view.

☛ *Go to Section 6.*

14

The rasp of a match being struck, followed by a *woosh*, suggests the paraffin has been ignited. Soon the entire house will be ablaze.

Even now a substantial part of your mind is clinical and detached. Within the space of a minute, you have evaluated and revaluated your prospects of escaping. You conclude that the situation is hopeless and decide to expend no further energy fighting the inevitable. The realisation that the smoke will most likely put an end to you before the flames touch your flesh is strangely calming.

You are aware that Mrs Hudson is in a state of panic so you put an arm around her shoulder and tell her what an exemplary landlady she has been and how her curried chicken is unsurpassed in all of London. This soothing equivocation seems to have the desired effect as the fumes enter your lungs and the world's greatest detective prepares for...

THE END

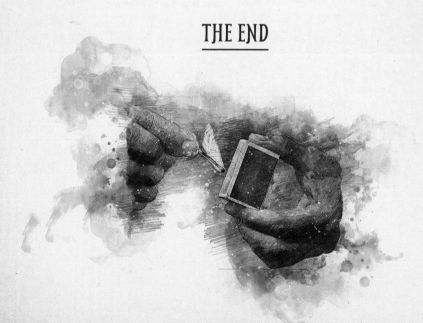

15

'Sherlock,' says your brother by way of a greeting, 'I wasn't expecting you today.'

'Events have escalated somewhat and I have further need of your assistance.'

You give Mycroft the details of Moriarty's recent visit and the subsequent attempts on your life. He gives you his undivided attention, unblemished by astonishment or concern for your well-being.

'All that remains is my personal testimony,' you say in conclusion. 'Moriarty is acting under the belief that, by silencing me, the case against him will be null and void.'

'Why did you not disabuse him of that belief?'

'Because I wish to be the focus of his attention, even as I bring his iniquitous world crashing down around him. While your nets gather up the shoals of smaller fish, I shall be the bait that catches the shark.'

'A delightful metaphor. You are aware that he has assassins everywhere and your theatrics will probably get you killed?'

'I shall lead them a merry dance. Could you arrange two tickets from Victoria to Paris later this evening, and safe passage to the station for the good doctor?'

'You're embroiling John Watson in this escapade?' Mycroft groans. 'Very well. I shall drive him myself.'

'The game is afoot, brother!' you cry with a forced glee that he will doubtless interpret as hysteria.

What now?

☛ *Lie low at Mycroft's for a few hours then visit Dr Watson? Go to Section 2.*

☛ *Return to Baker Street? Go to Section 34.*

16

You recall Irene Adler-Norton's warning not to return home and wonder why you did not heed it.

In desperation you rain blows against the immovable cellar doors, until the sound of Mrs Hudson's sobbing convinces you to take a more stoical approach.

☞ *Go to Section 14.*

17

The carriage draws to a halt and you realise that you are 20 yards from your brother Mycroft's Pall Mall residence.

'I hope we meet again under less anxious circumstances, Mr Holmes,' says Irene Adler-Norton as you step onto the pavement.

☛ *Go to Mycroft's house in Section 15.*

18

The Reichenbach Falls are as impressive as Herr Steiler insisted. Seven rocky steps create a cascade with a total drop of over 800 feet. The icy torrent sends up a mighty spray that looks like billowing smoke as it smashes into the coal-black rocks. The ceaseless roar of water is like the voice of an ancient god.

Staring into this surging abyss, you lose all sense of time but, when you come back to the present, you notice that Watson is talking to a local lad. Evidently a messenger. He reads the letter in his hand carefully before conveying its contents to you.

'It is from Herr Steiler. A lady from England has just arrived at the Englischer Hof. She is in the last stage of consumption but refuses to see a Swiss physician. He begs me to come as a personal favour. She is not expected to last the night.'

Watson implores you to return to Meiringen with him. You are about to consent when you glance at the young messenger. For the briefest instant he returns your gaze, conveying an entirely different message.

'I shall linger here a while longer Watson, then make my way to Rosenlaui as planned. Meet me there this evening.'

'I can show you the way to Rosenlaui,' offers the boy.

'No doubt,' you reply coldly. 'Go, Watson. All will be well.'

Watson looks perplexed but his sense of duty takes precedence. You watch his departure along the rocky path until he disappears from view.

You turn to the boy, who stares at you with frightened eyes.

'He is coming,' he says, then takes to his heels and disappears back down the track.

Are you ready to face your Nemesis?

☞ *If you are, go to Section 25.*

☞ *If you would rather flee and live to sleuth another day, go to Section 8.*

19

Your recent brush with death must have addled your memory. Go to the table and follow the link for the word 'sedate'. Remember to employ your celebrated powers of observation in future!

☞ *Go to Section 50.*

20

Your train pulls into Canterbury and waits at the station. This scheduled delay will not be a long one but will give Moriarty time to close the gap if your instincts are correct.

'We shall have to abandon our luggage Watson,' you say, exiting the carriage. The doctor follows but cannot hide his vexation at the loss of his travelling wardrobe.

'What now?' he asks as you watch the train depart.

'The cross-country to Newhaven arrives in an hour, then we continue over to Dieppe.'

Watson is about to vocalise an objection when you draw his attention to the distant smoke of a rapidly approaching single-coach engine.

You quickly hide yourselves behind a pile of luggage as the special roars past the station.

'Moriarty?' asks Watson with widening eyes.

'Indeed. He is now on his way to Paris. There is no doubt that we have avoided a murderous encounter.'

An hour later your train arrives and you are soon on your way to the Newhaven-Dieppe ferry.

☞ *Continue to Section 7.*

21

'I didn't know you had connections in Bavaria, Holmes,' remarks Watson, supping a modest mug of foamy local beer.

'I'm quite certain I have none,' you respond.

He looks puzzled, shakes his head and returns his attention to the beverage.

It can only be a matter of time before Moriarty tracks you to Munich. You leave your beer untouched and sink into melancholy thoughts before concluding that you should leave immediately.

☛ *You decide to continue to Switzerland. Go to Section 47.*

22

Irene Adler-Norton climbs into a luxurious, enclosed, four-wheeled carriage and signals you to follow her. Once inside the driver flicks his reins and you are away.

The characteristic growl of the Clarence's wheels ensures that not even the driver will overhear your conversation. You decide to take the initiative: 'I thank you for your timely intervention but I must confess to some surprise.'

'Surprising the great Sherlock Holmes is a reward in itself,' she interjects with a smile. 'You doubtless assumed that the *Illuminati* would take some pleasure in your demise?'

You nod.

'Well, I am afraid I cannot disabuse you of that notion. I am not here as their representative. They have aligned themselves with Professor Moriarty because you turned down their offer of employment.'

'And they wish to punish me for the rebuff.'

'Not at all. They have simply extended the very same offer to the professor. He will be their London agent.'

☛ *Now you know who is really pulling the strings, you can change the course of events by bookmarking the table in Section 51.*

☛ △ *Take the cab to Section 15.*

23

'Keeping secrets at this juncture is absurd!' Mycroft remarks coldly. 'Given the nature of your work, you must understand their importance better than most. I assure you that I am not being deliberately mysterious. There are other lives at stake in this affair.'

'Very well. I shall continue with our plan to close down Moriarty's organisation. What will you do next?'

'Moriarty is fixated on silencing me, like a predator stalking its prey. I shall lead him away from his natural habitat. Could you arrange passage to the continent for two?'

'Your companion?'

'Why, Dr Watson, of course.'

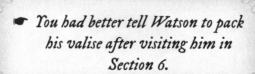

☞ *You had better tell Watson to pack his valise after visiting him in Section 6.*

24

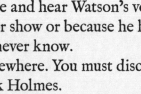

Watson has separated from the search party and, when he is close enough to your position, you call out to him.

He can barely conceal his delight at finding you alive but seems to comprehend the situation and makes no outward sign of having discovered you.

'What are you going to do, Holmes?' he asks.

'Moriarty's men are still at large. I propose to remain on the continent for a while. I would implore you to let the world believe that Sherlock Holmes perished here this day.'

'Of course. Will I see you again?'

'Indubitably, my dear Watson. The moment I return to London, I shall let you know.'

You crawl away from the ledge and hear Watson's voice calling, 'Holmes? Holmes?' Whether for show or because he had something further to say to you, you may never know.

For now, your destiny lies elsewhere. You must discover whether this world has a use for Sherlock Holmes.

THE END

25

A dark figure appears on the path, tall and thin and moving with a determined energy.

'The time is at hand,' growls Professor Moriarty.

You assess the situation and feel as if your powers of deduction have been heightened by the Alpine air. The conclusion you reach is irrefutable: these really could be the final moments of your life.

'I have one request,' you say.

'Name it.'

'I should like to write a note for my companion.'

He nods. You remove a pen and notepaper from your pack.

If you are to perish today, you are determined to ensure that Moriarty does not see another. You leave instructions for Watson to find the detailed files on Moriarty's organisation, which you bid him pass on to the police. Unable to resist showing off, you also let him know that you knew the message from Herr Steiler was a hoax. Finally, you find some words of sincere fraternal affection before signing off.

You put the letter into your silver cigarette case, which you place on a flat rock. Then you stretch your limbs, turn to the professor and let him know that you are ready to do battle. Standing with your back to the Grand Reichenbach Fall, you prepare to meet your greatest enemy.

In all things Professor Moriarty is the great deceiver. His gangly academic countenance belies a wiry strength and more than a passing familiarity with unarmed fighting styles. He does not waste time testing your defences but hurls himself at you like a frenzied beast.

You had not expected a gentlemanly boxing match - he wants to get his claw-like fingers around your throat and choke the life from you!

What is your response?

☞ *Allow him to get closer.*
Go to Section 32.

☞ △ *Keep him at a distance.*
Go to Section 40.

26

You are still alive and unharmed! Surely they could not have missed at almost point-blank range. The shooter appears to be speaking but the ringing in your ears renders the words unintelligible.

Your wits return like a rush of blood and you notice two facts at once: the shooter is a woman and the cudgel-wielding brute is no longer looming behind you. You turn around to confirm your suspicion: he is lying very still on the dirty cobblestones.

'Mr Holmes?' she says with the voice of a confident, self-reliant woman, who handles a firearm with the dexterity of a trained soldier.

Do you know anyone like that?

☛ *No, I must be suffering from memory loss.* Go to Section 30.

☛ *Yes, I was a witness at her wedding!* Go to Section 38.

☛ *Yes, she's a member of the secret society who recruited me.* Go to Section 33.

☛ *Yes, I double-crossed her and her organisation.* Go to Section 22.

27

As the thug raises his cudgel to pulverise your skull, you take to your heels.

Despite his size he is surprisingly fast and frighteningly tenacious. The streets are strangely abandoned, as if the people of London have been paid off by Moriarty to offer you no succour.

You spot the entrance to a narrow alley and calculate that it will lead to a more populated area, where your assailant might be less confident of committing murder in broad daylight.

The passage is dark and filthy. You are roughly in the middle when another figure appears at the other end. Something about its posture tells you that it is no innocent bystander.

You are trapped.

What will you do?

☛ *Turn back and face your pursuer?*
Go to Section 37.

☛ *Or charge towards the newcomer?*
Go to Section 5.

You enter Victoria Station, dressed as a priest. The disguise attracts some attention, but no suspicion, and you deflect questions from the staff by waving your first-class ticket and responding with an exuberant but incomprehensible approximation of Italian.

Finally, you take your seat in the second carriage of the Continental Express and, having the compartment all to yourself, wait in quiet contemplation.

A familiar voice from the platform draws your attention. A guard opens the door to your carriage and asks the new passenger, 'Do you speak Italian, by any chance?'

'Not a word,' replies Watson as he climbs aboard.

You sense Watson's befuddled appraisal before he takes his seat and you are pleased that not a glimmer of recognition crosses his face, even when your eyes meet. The crash of closing doors is punctuated by a piercing whistle, signalling your imminent departure. A perfect time for you to say, 'My dear Watson, you have not even condescended to say good morning.'

Even with the prospect of being murdered by Moriarty's assassins, you can still derive pleasure from surprising your friend. But it is a short-lived pleasure. At that very moment your adversary appears on the platform and makes for the train. He is seconds too late, however. The guard is unmoved by the professor's remonstrance and the train begins to pull away in a cloud of smoke.

Watson watches the indignant, angular figure until he disappears from view.

'Are we really fleeing from such a man?' he asks.

You hand him the morning paper by way of a reply, nodding understandingly as he reads the headline and the colour drains from his face.

'Holmes, they've set fire to 221b Baker Street! Is Mrs Hudson—?'
'She is unharmed. But Moriarty is in earnest, Watson. He evidently knows that we boarded this train and will doubtless engage a special to catch up with us.'

☛ *If you think it wise to get off at the next convenient station, go to Section 20.*

☛ 👁 *If you would prefer to stay on the train, go to Section 9.*

29

Tiny slivers of light break into the pitch blackness of the coal cellar as the fire outside takes hold. The crackle of flame and stench of paraffin are quickly overwhelmed by a thick smoke that you feel, rather than see, in the darkness.

You do your best to calm Mrs Hudson, who is on the edge of hysteria. The only thing you feel is the shame of being so easily outmanoeuvred. If you are to perish in this pitiful pyre, you are resolved to do so with defiant dignity.

With one arm around your trembling landlady, you close your eyes and take your mind to a place first shown to you by eastern mystics.

'Good God, man, help me move this!'

The voice from outside the coal cellar brings you back to the material universe and you start to choke.

Infernal light blazes as the doors are flung open and two men, sensibly equipped with scarves to cover their noses and mouths, help you and Mrs Hudson out of the cellar, through the smoke-filled hall and into the deliciously pungent air of Baker Street.

You recognise one of your rescuers as Godfrey Norton, husband of your erstwhile adversary-cum-protector Irene Adler Norton. He helps you into a carriage, reassures you that Mrs Hudson will be taken care of and offers you a flask of beer, which you gratefully accept. Through watering eyes you are aware of

another passenger - it is John Watson, who offers only a concerned, baffled smile.

'It is imperative that you both get out of England immediately,' says Godfrey Norton.

'Of course,' replies the doctor. 'Mycroft has arranged passage to the continent.'

Consciousness starts to fade again. Was there something in the beer?

You do not feel any immediate threat so you allow yourself to slip into a welcome slumber.

☞ *Wake up in Section 4.*

30

'You have my gratitude, madam,' you say.

'You do not know me, Mr Holmes?'

'I regret to say that I do not.'

'I understand you. And thank you for keeping my secrets. You are in great danger, Mr Sherlock Holmes, and you ought to leave London as soon as possible.'

A hansom is waiting in the street behind the lady. She gestures for you to climb aboard. 'Go to your brother, Mr Holmes. He has been a good friend to Godfrey and me.'

And with that, the enigmatic woman disappears into the street and is lost in the bustle.

☞ Take the cab to Pall Mall in Section 15.

31

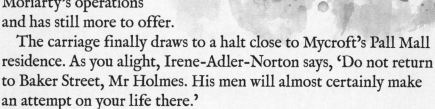

Can you trust her? She had the opportunity to end your life in the alley or simply allow the brute to beat you to death. The involvement of the *Illuminati* certainly complicates things.

For now, you decide to put the secret order to the back of your mind and focus on your immediate problems. Mrs Adler-Norton confirms that she is the source of the intelligence on Moriarty's operations and has still more to offer.

The carriage finally draws to a halt close to Mycroft's Pall Mall residence. As you alight, Irene-Adler-Norton says, 'Do not return to Baker Street, Mr Holmes. His men will almost certainly make an attempt on your life there.'

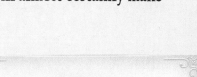

☞ *Go to Section 15.*

32

Moriarty has made another rare mistake and allowed his hatred to quash his judgement. You let him get close but then evade his grasping hands at the last moment and use his own momentum to unbalance him.

Even as he loses his footing on the slippery ledge, his eyes blaze with loathing, almost demanding that you fall to your doom with him. And then he is gone, borne on the icy deluge to the dark rocks below. A single faint but sickening slap confirms that the Napoleon of Crime is no more.

As you stare into the chasm, your mind races. Moriarty is vanquished and his London organisation has been destroyed but the acolytes who followed him to Europe are still at large.

It is time to make a crucial decision.

☛ *Would you allow the world to think you perished with Moriarty? Go to Section 35.*

☛ △ *Or would you rather reunite with Watson? Go to Section 49.*

33

A Clarence is waiting at the junction with the passage. The ornate, four-wheeled carriage looks quite out of place on the ramshackle street. Irene Adler-Norton climbs aboard and invites you to join her.

When the doors are closed, the cab sets off at a sedate pace and you are able to converse with assured privacy.

'I wish I could bring you happy news, Mr Holmes. But the fact of the matter is that the *Illuminati* wish for Professor Moriarty to remain at large and will not help you against him.'

'Why would a society committed to science and reason support such a man?'

'They believe criminal organisations to be an unavoidable facet of metropolitan life and wish such organisations to be ruled by men of reason.'

'Will they help him against me?'

'The majority believe it would be dishonourable to do so after you aided them, and so remain neutral.'

'And you?'

'I owe you my life, Mr Holmes. I cannot stand by and watch you be cut down.'

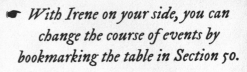

☛ *With Irene on your side, you can change the course of events by bookmarking the table in Section 50.*

☛ △ *The carriage takes you to Section 19.*

34

Returning to Baker Street is risky; Moriarty has already proven he can break in, even while you are at home. When you arrive, 221b appears to be empty.

You look for Mrs Hudson but can find no trace of her until you hear muffled sobs coming from the coal cellar.

Flinging open the doors, you enter the small, dark room and find your terrified landlady bound and gagged in the corner.

'Mrs Hudson!'

As you move to untie her bonds, you realise too late that she was trying to signal with her eyes.

There is a movement behind you and a sudden pain that spreads across the back of your head. Sparks of light invade your vision and you lose consciousness for a moment.

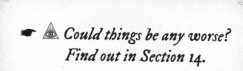

You rise groggily to your feet, just as the cellar doors slam shut, plunging the room into complete darkness. There is a loud crash. Someone has evidently blocked the doors with something heavy, confirmed when you attempt to open them.

You find your way to Mrs Hudson's struggling form and remove her gag.

There is a distinct sound of liquid sluicing in the hall and then a sharp smell assails your nostrils: paraffin!

☞ ⚠ *Could things be any worse?*
Find out in Section 14.

35

The ground surrounding the falls is wet and you have left obvious tracks. Retracing your own steps backwards is an option that you immediately reject as imprecise and time consuming. Then you notice that the rocky wall, which at first glance seemed completely sheer, has small ledges and handholds that might allow you to exit the location without leaving a trace.

You do not permit yourself time to consider the raging torrent and rocks below but start to climb the slippery stone. Beneath you the roaring chasm seems to change in tone, as if the voice of Moriarty was screaming up at you from the depths of Hades.

Several times you slip, certain it will be the last misstep you ever make but, after a long, nerve-racking ascent, you heave yourself

over a ridge and find yourself lying on your back and breathing in great relieved sobs on a ledge covered in soft moss. A penthouse at Brown's could not have afforded a more welcome luxury.

When your breathing is back under control, you peer back over the edge and see the unmistakable figure of Dr Watson, accompanied by members of the local constabulary. You watch them locate the waterlogged body of Professor Moriarty, then your walking stick and cigarette case. You are relieved when Watson opens the latter and extracts your letter.

You can only imagine your friend's distress. The urge to call out to him, to let him know that you still live, is so strong that you force yourself to get to your feet and leave the scene without a backwards glance.

Does the world still have a use for Sherlock Holmes? Perhaps the answer lies outside the smoky confines of London. It is time to find out.

THE END

36

The route to Rosenlaui passes through breathtaking Alpine scenery. Your destination is a hamlet with a population of only several dozen, many of whom tend livestock in the mountains.

You are happy to discover that the single guesthouse has a vacant double room and grateful to get an early night after a day hiking along the gorge.

The next morning you wake to bright sunshine and, finding the hamlet deserted, walk to the well to slake your thirst with refreshing local water.

You stare down the deep shaft into the sun-dappled liquid and are only dimly aware of a figure approaching. Turning, you expect to see Dr Watson but are horrified to meet the twin pools of insanity that are the eyes of Professor Moriarty!

His long fingers find your throat, simultaneously attempting to squeeze the air from your lungs and thrust you into the well.

At that moment you realise it is time to be of use to mankind. Without you there is every chance Moriarty will escape justice. If you are to perish, it is imperative that the professor does so too.

Perhaps realising your determination, Moriarty loosens his fingers but you grasp his wrists and allow your combined weight to carry you over the stone edge of the well.

You crash into the water, maintaining your iron grip on your struggling foe. Deeper and deeper you fall into the liquid darkness. You ensure that your enemy has surrendered his foul existence to it before it fills your lungs.

There is no fear in your heart; only satisfaction that you have resolved your final problem.

THE END

37

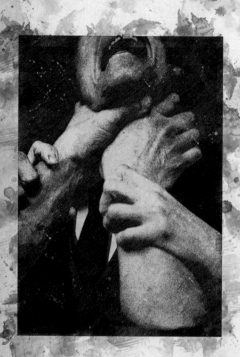

You run back the way you came and the brute stops suddenly, possibly not expecting you to take the initiative. A cudgel is an effective weapon but only if you have room to use it. The brute is forced to use an overhead swing, which leaves his entire body open. You land a punch under his chin and a rather ungentlemanly kick to a sensitive part, causing him to double in pain.

Not waiting for him to recover, you attempt to barge past the man but he drops the cudgel and grabs your coat with an enormous, calloused hand, pulling you back and then bearing down on you like a great bloodthirsty bear.

With both hands secured around your neck, the brute starts to squeeze. His grip is an iron vice that your ineffective blows can do nothing to weaken. A roaring fills your skull and darkness closes as you are denied even a single life-sustaining gasp.

Your oxygen-starved brain conjures the sound of hellish hooves. Could it be an apocalyptic horseman coming to claim your soul?

☞ *Go to Section 42 to find out.*

38

'Mrs Irene Adler-Norton if I am not mistaken. I thought you had fled to the continent.'

'I thought I was fleeing for my life, Mr Holmes, but now I fear yours is in greater danger.'

'As evinced by recent events. I thank you for your timely intervention and for the intelligence you provided on Professor Moriarty.'

'You saved my life, Mr Holmes. Perhaps we might consider our accounts settled?'

You nod.

She gestures to a hansom cab that waits in the street beyond the alley. 'The driver will take you to Pall Mall. Your brother resides there, does he not?'

You are no longer surprised by her near-omniscience and politely accept the offer.

☞ *Make use of the ride to collect your thoughts and visit Mycroft in Section 15.*

39

'At first we thought it an elaborate hoax or a ridiculous attempt to revive a cabal that died out a century ago. But it appears that a secretive foreign agency has taken an interest in Professor Moriarty's schemes.'

'Which brings the matter under your jurisdiction.'

'Indeed.'

'This group operates without the knowledge of the Bavarian state. Any overt investigation by Her Majesty's government would be viewed as a provocation.'

'Allow me to cut to the chase, brother: you wish me to go to Bavaria?'

Mycroft takes a sip of his brandy.

'Switzerland, actually. And we can't offer you any men.'

'I only need one.'

☞ *You'll find him in Section 6.*

40

You have studied the French fighting art known as *savate*, which employs both fists and feet. It has many merits but is not ideally suited to combat on a slippery ledge above a raging waterfall.

You deliver a sharp kick to Moriarty's solar plexus but his fury overcomes the shock of pain and he traps your foot in the crook of his elbow. With a feral snarl he prepares to hurl you to your doom, but too late realises that he has also lost his own balance.

Time seems to stop and you find yourself in space, suspended in the frozen deluge above the lethal black rocks. Moriarty's face is a portrait of indignation and abject hatred.

You are able to contemplate the futility of your situation. The world is about to lose two of its greatest minds because providence saw fit to put those minds in opposition.

Alpine sunlight transforms the Reichenbach Falls into a million glowing diamonds, and you fancy you will have time to count each and every one of them.

And then it will be ...

THE END

41

Paris is sprawling, noisy, debauched and dilapidated - you feel quite at home. Or at least you would if you were not being pursued by a murderous monster. You decide to have a stroll along the Seine to clear your head.

In a riverside market you realise that you are being watched. You agree with Watson to split up, to confound your pursuers individually and make your separate ways back to the hotel.

Deftly sidestepping into a colourful tent, you find yourself in the incense-infused parlour of a fortune teller.

A voice asks in French, 'Would you know your destiny?' It comes from the only other occupant, a richly robed and made-up woman. She is seated behind a table festooned with candles, tarot cards and a large crystal ball.

There is a familiar tang to the incense, you feel your head swim not unpleasantly.

You shake your head. 'No thank you.'

'This is not a sanctuary,' she replies in accented English. 'Take a seat or be gone.'

You take a seat.

'You will soon have a meeting with fate and, whatever happens, do not run from it. You must abandon friends and go into the world to make a difference.'

'If only you could really see the future,' you scoff, enjoying the musky ambiance.

Her eyes glaze over and she intones mysteriously, 'Everyone will carry a tiny telegraph machine and spend every waking hour staring into it, like stupid fish caught in a net.'

The heavily opiated air has clearly rotted her mind. Perhaps you can turn this to your advantage. 'May I purchase your costume?' you ask, fumbling with your purse.

You give the woman all the money in your possession and, a few minutes later, stumble from her tent outlandishly disguised.

When you arrive at the hotel, Watson cannot speak for almost half an hour through tears of mirth.

☞ *That's quite enough frivolity.*
Your next destination is
Switzerland. Go to Section 47.

42

You hear a jarring 'crack' - the sound of a tubular object constructed from the hardwood *lignum vitae* being forcefully applied to a human cranium if you are not mistaken.

The brute's eyes roll back into his head, the crushing pressure ceases and the strangler collapses in a heavily muscled heap. The constable who administered the truncheon blow steps into view.

He is joined by another policeman, who checks the brute is still breathing. A third figure joins you in the dirty alleyway - it is your brother Mycroft.

'Where did the other one go?' you ask groggily.

'There was only one,' says Mycroft brusquely. 'Honestly, Sherlock, must you always exaggerate your exploits?'

The constable helps you to your feet and into a carriage waiting in the adjoining street. Your brother joins you and signals for the driver to depart.

You remain silent for the duration of the journey to Mycroft's Pall Mall residence. Only when you are alone in his drawing room and nursing a welcome brandy do you say, 'Professor Moriarty evidently wishes to prevent my testimony.'

Mycroft stares into his own untouched brandy. 'He may not be the only one.'

He produces a small slip of card and hands it to you. It contains a hand-drawn sigil - an open eye surrounded by a triangle.

'Does this mean anything to you?' he asks.

It is vital that you give your brother an honest answer.

☞ 'Nothing.' Go to Section 39.

☞ 🔺 'The sigil of a group that has declared itself my enemy.' Go to Section 51 and reference this location.

☞ 🔺 'A friend, whose sole protection is secrecy.' Go to Section 50 and reference a key word from this location.

43

You shout down from the top of the falls and, eventually, one of the search party points towards you. Watson runs towards the incline, his delight evident from his gait.

However, when you are finally reunited, there is concern as well as relief in your friend's eyes.

The constables close in and one of them lays an apprehending hand on your shoulder.

In heavily accented English he says, 'Mr Sherlock Holmes, I am arresting you for the murder of Professor Moriarty.'

As you are led back to Meiringen, you realise that the *Illuminati* have orchestrated this situation. Without his network Moriarty is no longer of any use, and you have rid them of an inconvenience.

If you wish to avoid the noose, you will doubtless have to renegotiate with these shadowy puppeteers. For now, you must allow yourself to be treated like a common criminal.

THE END

44

Taking a step backwards puts you on the very edge of the precipice. Behind you there is only the unholy roar of the falls and certain death on the rocks far below.

You shout to ensure Moriarty can hear your words.

'The *Illuminati* are dedicated to progress and you were nothing more than an unsavoury puppet to them. Without your gang what use are you? They will simply cut your strings, professor!'

Moriarty's expression changes from surprise at your mention of his prospective employers to renewed rage at the slight. He hurls himself at you again, utterly heedless of the danger.

At the last moment you step to the side and slip through his grasp, using the fighting art known as baritsu. The professor makes a desperate attempt to grasp you with his long fingers and drag you down to the depths of hell. And then he is gone.

It takes you many minutes to recover your composure and fully comprehend that you have vanquished your greatest adversary.

But now it is time to decide.

☛ *Would you allow the world to think you perished with Moriarty? Go to Section 35.*

☛ ⚠ *Or would you rather reunite with Watson? Go to Section 49.*

45

'They claim to be continuing the work of a secret society that was founded in Bavaria a century ago. Apparently, they wish to extend their influence in London by helping Professor Moriarty maintain his position.'

'The *Illuminati*?'

'You are aware of them? I suppose I should not be surprised - their attempt to recruit me was hardly subtle.'

'This may present us with the opportunity to rid ourselves of two evils.'

'I take your meaning, brother. I had already planned to lead Moriarty away from London by fleeing to the continent. Perhaps I can also convince this cabal that their man is an unsuitable candidate.'

'It will be a very dangerous undertaking. You are already a marked man.'

'As I explained to the professor when he turned up unannounced this morning, danger is part of my trade.'

'Very well. I can arrange your passage for tomorrow.'

'I shall need two sets of tickets. Dr Watson will be accompanying me on this trip.'

☞ *You had better let Watson know in Section 6.*

The *Illuminati* are dedicated to the promotion of reason and not known for a propensity to violence. Nevertheless, they believe you to have betrayed their trust and you cannot take your safety for granted here in their historic birthplace.

Your arrival was evidently noted the very second that you set foot on Bavarian soil, and you soon find yourself in the company of a group of expressionless men who insist you be blindfolded before meeting their leader. It is a little late to retreat so you consent.

When the covering is removed from your eyes, you are in the familiar surroundings of a masonic lodge. The man before you nods for his cohorts to leave before introducing himself as 'Brother Spartacus'.

'What brings you to Munich, Mr Sherlock Holmes?' he asks.

'I would petition you to reconsider bringing Professor Moriarty into your order.'

'And why would we do that?'

'Because I have found a better candidate to manage organised crime in London.'

'Professor Moriarty's moral compass may be cracked but his intellect is second to none. Who do you propose?'

'I propose myself and I challenge your assessment of his intellect.'

Spartacus smiles broadly. 'And why should the order trust you, Mr Holmes? you have already betrayed us once before.'

Brother Spartacus

'If I crossed you, it was only because my moral compass was intact. But perhaps my initial assessment of your order was misguided.'

'I cannot lie: we greatly covet your peculiar talents. Give me time to convene our council and we shall give you our decision.'

The look of triumph in Brother Spartacus's eyes leaves you in no doubt as to which way he will vote.

You keep your face expressionless.

Only a day ago you were pondering your usefulness. But Sherlock Holmes, Crime King of London?

THE END

47

Switzerland seems a perfect place to seek sanctuary. After the defeat of Napoleon 76 years ago, it declared itself neutral in all military and political conflicts.

You refuse to let down your guard until Moriarty is behind bars but the Rhone Valley and the majestic snow-covered Alps have a soothing effect on your nerves and on those of your stalwart companion.

On Sunday, 3 May you reach the village of Meiringen, where you put up at the Englischer Hof. The landlord is one Peter Steiler, a former waiter at the Grosvenor in London, who has an excellent command of English. You decide to make this your headquarters while you explore the surrounding area.

The following morning you prepare to set off for the hamlet of Rosenlaui, where you hope to spend the night. You meet Herr Steiler in the lobby and he greets you cordially.

After learning of your destination, he effuses, 'Oh, Mr Holmes, you cannot possibly go to Rosenlaui without making a small detour to see the falls of Reichenbach!'

His enthusiasm for this natural wonder is infectious but, for some reason, the name sends an unpleasant sensation down your spine. Are you becoming superstitious?

☞ *If you would like to visit the falls, go to Section 18.*

☞ *If you would prefer to go directly to Rosenlaui, go to Section 36.*

48

You retreat to the edge of the precipice and feel icy droplets stinging your neck. The falls roar like a beast and you glance down into the precipice where lethal black rocks wait.

Moriarty's rage is as cold as the spray. He closes the distance slowly but purposefully. He does not care about his own fate, you realise, provided he can take you with him.

Your powers of analysis are screaming - you have lost the advantage and the odds of you surviving this encounter are rapidly collapsing.

And then a shot rings out. Moriarty takes three steps forward like a marionette, his face a frozen mask of rage, then he topples and plunges into the roaring deluge.

From a ledge overlooking the fall, you hear a familiar voice, feminine, confident.

'Mr Sherlock Holmes, I believe you are now in my debt. Dr Watson will be returning soon with members of the local constabulary. If you linger, you will be charged with Moriarty's murder.'

'The man is a wanted criminal!' you protest as Irene Adler-Norton comes into view.

'It will make little difference. His brother, Colonel James Moriarty, has considerable influence. You must allow the world to believe you have perished together, at least until the evidence against him has become incontrovertible.'

You locate some hand and footholds and gracelessly propel yourself up onto the ledge. She offers you a gloved hand and you find yourself kneeling before her like a suitor.'

'Very well, Mrs Norton. What now?'

'Why, Mr Holmes, the whole world could use the talents of a consulting detective!'

THE END

49

'Watson!' you call from the top of the falls and fancy you hear your voice echo in the gorge.

'Holmes!' The doctor's joyous response seems to fill the Alpine landscape.

You make your way back down the rocky elevation as quickly as you are able. And then something brings you to a halt.

Click-click-click ... click! A metallic, mechanical sound, out of place among the rocks and water.

Watson is perhaps 50 yards away but you see his eyes widen with alarm.

Another sound, almost muted by the waterfall: a powerful explosion of air.

One moment Watson is standing, full of life and enthusiasm. Then he is lying on the Swiss grass, motionless.

You hurry to your companion but it takes agonising minutes to find a safe path. When you finally reach his side, he is barely breathing.

'Holmes ...' he says again. It is his final word.

The other members of his party have taken cover or else are searching the ridge for signs of the assassin. As you look into the motionless face of your good friend, you feel something hot and wet roll down your cheek. You have no doubt that he would have delighted in such a display.

Whatever happens now, you can be of no further use to Dr John Watson.

THE END

50

Come to this section when you see the *Illuminati* symbol to determine your true path.

Codeword	Go to	Codeword	Go to
BRANDY	Section 23	*HURLS*	Section 48
MILE	Section 12	*FAINT*	Section 24
SPARKS	Section 29	*SEDATE*	Section 17
CLOUD	Section 4	*UNHOLY*	Section 24

51

Come to this section when you see the *Illuminati* symbol to determine your true path.

Section 15	Section 42	Section 14	Section 9	Section 21	Section 40	Section 49
Section 31	Section 45	Section 16	Section 41	Section 46	Section 44	Section 43

PICTURE CREDITS

The publishers would like to thank the following sources for their kind permission to reproduce the pictures in this book.

Alamy: Allan Cash Picture Library 45. **Getty Images:** Laurent Hamels 204; Holgs 93, 113; Meshaphoto 116, 131, 147; Zoranm 123, 143. **Pexels:** Cottonbro 158; Charles Parker 146. **Pixabay:** 20, 176; Jazella 187. **PublicDomainPictures:** George Hodan 126. **PxHere:** 12, 30. **Shutterstock:** Africa Studio 80BL; Akaiser 53, 60, 77, 170; Akamakis 79BL, 111, 133, 141; Aksenova Natalya 66; ANL 154T, 191; Aodaodaodaod 201; ArtFamily 197T, 212L; Maria Avvakumova 21, 42, 193; William Barton 177, 195; Jill Battaglia 164; Jule Berlin 78TL, 102, 140TR; F. J. Carneros 6R, 59, 222; James Clarke 95, 97, 132; Ysbrand Cosijn 6B, 25, 40, 55, 61, 62, 73, 78TR, 118, 138, 144, 150, 154BR, 159, 174, 180, 184TL, 184BR, 186; Mr Dasenna 9, 17, 27TR, 34, 88, 140BL, 162, 182, 185; Denny George 179, 220; Djawings 65; Dragon Images 166; Duntrune Studios 79T, 109, 135; Eillen 10; EML 78B, 130; Everett Collection 200; Faestock 32, 50, 57, 64, 69, 155B, 183; Ffolas 155T, 173; Martin Fowler 6T, 31; Georgiy M 169; Glasshouse Images 160; Lukas Gojda 68, 154BL, 161; IgorGolovniov 26, 163, 206TR, 213; Michael C. Gray 81, 100, 153; Gresei 103; Gyvafoto 188; Heijo 22; Inked Pixels 19; Maria Isaeva 58, 87; Juri V 128; Giorgos Karagiannis 47; Karjalas 133; KathySG 79BR, 117, 120, 125, 171, 214; Jakub Krechowicz 7, 41, 44, 74, 82, 104, 137; Kryzhov 84, 106, 108, 122; Sergey Ksen 92; Andrey Kuzmin 36, 76; Chris Lawrence Travel 29; LightField Studios 14; AlexanderLipko 35, 43, 192; Loocmill 83, 91; Lvaleriy 54, 71; Adam Machovsky 129; Madlen 63; Mega Pixel 96, 105, 134; Nasidastudio 200; Naskami 199; New Africa 8, 23, 49, 56, 85, 89, 90, 99, 110, 114, 145, 206BL, 209; Volodymyr Nikitenko 187; Nito 194, 205; Stephen Orsillo 121; Pegasus Pics 115, 211; Peyker 210; Photomak 188; Preto Perola 46, 51, 70; Valeriya Popova 221B; Pterwort 16; Pummyoohoo 52; Thomas Grant Readle 142, 148; Ripio 215; s-ts 80TR; Ev. Safronov 98, 152; Pete Saloutos 208; Smetana Natasha 156; Sommthink 27BL; Stephm2506 157; Subbotina Anna 13, 39T, 65, 67, 93, 113; Tarasyuk Igor 37TR; Chris Tefme 167, 189; TonelloPhotography 165; Tung Phan 172; Unique Vision 198; Peter Versnel 221BL; Jiri Vlcek 57; Wadas Jerzy 203. **Unsplash:** David Boca 127; Jesse Gardner 197, 212BL; Richard James 181; LSE Library 37BL; Angelo Pantazis 169; Annie Spratt 45, 207, 218; Trail 217. **WikiMedia Commons:** Medjai 107; The Portable Antiquities Scheme 15.

Every effort has been made to acknowledge correctly and contact the source and/or copyright holder of each picture any unintentional errors or omissions will be corrected in future editions of this book.